in my Father's House

in my Father's House

Finding Your Heart's True Home

MARY A. KASSIAN

with DALE McCLESKEY

BROADMAN
& HOLMAN
PUBLISHERS

NASHVILLE, TENNESSEE

Ten-digit ISBN: 0805430822
Thirteen-digit ISBN: 9780805430820

Published by Broadman & Holman Publishers,
Nashville, Tennessee

Dewey Decimal Classification: 231.1
Subject Heading: GOD \ FATHERS

1 2 3 4 5 6 7 8 9   10 09 08 07 06 05

To my father,
Ulrich Karl Thomas

CONTENTS ·

INTRODUCTION

DOES EVERY CHILD NEED A FATHER? Increasingly, our society's answer to this question is "no," or at least "not necessarily." In the past few years, several well-known actresses have announced their intentions to bear and raise children alone. A recent *Time* magazine proposed that remaining unmarried can be "incredibly empowering" for women—even when this choice involves raising children without the presence of a father. The article implied that no woman really *needs* a husband, and by extension, children do not necessarily *need* a father.

Children today become fatherless through promiscuity, abandonment, separation, and divorce, in the name of male "freedom" or female "empowerment." The net result is that tonight at least 40 percent of American children will go to sleep in homes in which their fathers do not live.[1]

We as a society have lost the presence of fathers, but we also have lost something much more fundamental: we have lost our idea of fatherhood. We are living in a culture of fatherlessness. Unlike earlier periods of father absence caused by war, we now face more than a physical loss affecting some homes. This cultural loss affects *every* home. Our society is afflicted not only with the absence of fathers but also with the absence of our *belief* in fathers.[2]

Few idea shifts in this century have had such enormous implications. At stake is who we are as male and female, what type of society we will become, and even more importantly, the way we understand and relate to God. Many people, inside as well as outside the church,

1

no longer believe in the fatherhood of God. Skeptical, hostile feelings toward men have translated into skeptical, hostile feelings toward the God who images himself as Father. But the need to be well fathered is a fundamental need of the human heart. It is a need that was put in our spirits by our Creator—the heavenly Father, the true Father—who alone defines what fatherhood means and what fatherhood was meant to be. Relating to God as Father is essential to our spiritual well-being and is central to what it means to be a believer.

God is our Father. That does not mean that God is male. He is Spirit. And he encompasses all that is good in masculinity and femininity. The Bible at times uses feminine analogies and metaphors when speaking of God's actions and attributes: He carried the nation Israel in his womb (Isa. 46:3). He cries out like a woman in labor (Isa. 42:14). He birthed the Jewish nation (Deut. 32:18). He has compassion on us like a mother has compassion for the baby at her breast (Isa. 49:13). He nurses and nurtures us (Ps. 131:2). He comforts as a mother comforts (Isa. 66:13). These and other passages exhibit the beautiful, tender, nurturing aspect of God's character.

Because of these motherlike analogies, many in the Christian community minimize or even deny the importance of the name *Father* for God. They argue that it is but one name among many, and given the times we live in, we ought not to regard it as his preferred name. They suggest that we call him "Mother," "Mother and Father," our "Heavenly Parent," or use nongender-specific names such as "Source" or "Creator." More and more people are beginning to object to the practice of using masculine pronouns for God.

Why do we call God "Father"? It is a question that demands an articulate biblical answer. The first and most obvious reason we call him Father is because that is what he wants to be called. The first person of the Trinity has many names—Almighty One, Creator, Most High, Holy Holy Holy, Rock, the Great I AM—but when Jesus came to tear away the veil so we could look directly into the heart of God, he revealed God as Father. Jesus used the word *Father* more than any other description or name. And he taught us to address God in the same way: "Our Father who art in heaven." *Father* is God's self-revealed designation.

What do you think of when you hear the word *Father*? I think of sitting perched on the splintery counter of my carpenter dad's dusty workshop, watching him work. I think of the pungent smell of fresh-cut wood. I think of his huge, strong, callused hands. I think of learning my multiplication tables by pounding groups of nails into a two-by-four. I think of the white doll cradle he built for my sixth birthday, the set of bedroom furniture he built for my twelfth birthday, and the basement renovation he helped me with last year. I think of being rescued in snowstorms, watching fireworks from the roof, folding paper stars at Christmas, and being tickled till my sides hurt.

Many people do not have good thoughts and feelings when they hear the word *father.* To them the word means "abandonment, anger, shame, insecurity, fear, unpredictability, conflict, or pain." But whether your thoughts are good or bad, it is undeniable that the word *father* means something to you. That's because *father* is a word that refers to someone. The concept is not abstract. When you speak of your father, you are speaking of a person who has, in one way or another, profoundly affected your life. He is someone who is or was alive—someone who has individual characteristics and a distinct personality, someone with whom you might interact and relate. Whether positive or negative, the word *father* means something real to each one of us. We all have a strong, clear concept of what *father* means—or what it ought to mean.

It is astounding that God would have us call him Father. The implications are staggering. The fact that he is Father indicates that he is a living, personal being and not an impersonal force. It means that we can get to know him. It means that we can talk to him and interact with him. It means that we can relate to him on a personal and even an intimate basis. I might not know how to relate to an Almighty One, a Most High, or the Great I AM because I have not met anybody like that. I have no earthly frame of reference to do so. But relating to a Father? That's different. *Father* does not denote an abstract force, a metaphysical power, or a cosmic aura. It speaks of a person with a distinct personality and characteristics. God would have us call him Father because it is a personal term that refers to a personal being with whom we can personally relate.

Father is also the term that best describes God's relationships, who he is in relationship to others. God relates to his only begotten Son, Jesus, and to us, his adopted children, as Father. *Father* implies family interaction. It implies causality and dependency, for a father is the source of life. It implies love and intimacy. It implies certain roles and responsibilities. Father is the pacesetter. He is the initiator, visionary, boundary setter, source, and final authority. A good father is committed to his family. He loves, protects, and provides. He lovingly guides, corrects, teaches, and instructs his children. A father also bequeaths an inheritance upon his children.

Consider Father God's relationship with his Son, Jesus. The Father has greater authority than Christ (John 12:16; 14:28; 17:2). Though equal in essence, Jesus submits himself to the Father's will (Phil. 2:6–8). The Father sent Jesus to secure redemption on our behalf (John 3:16–17; 17:3). Jesus always does what pleases his Father (John 8:29). Jesus follows his Father's directives exactly (John 14:31). He learns from his Father (John 15:15), speaks his Father's words (John 8:28; 14:24; 17:8), does his Father's work (John 10:25; 14:10), and brings glory to his Father (John 14:13). The Father highly exalted his Son (Phil. 2:9; Heb. 5:7–10), and appointed him heir to all things (Heb. 1:2). Jesus is the rightful heir to everything that belongs to his Father (John 16:15). Everything that Jesus has comes from his Father (John 17:7, 22, 24).

The word *father* denotes a different type of relationship than the words *mother, brother, sister, aunt,* or *uncle.* It is the term that most accurately represents the nature of the relationship between the first and second persons of the Trinity. And it is the term that most accurately represents the nature of his relationship to us. God calls himself "Father" because the word characterizes his relationships better than any other word.

Father is the most significant name of the God of the Bible. It is the name that sets Christianity apart from all the other religions of the world. Other religions invite us to worship their gods, allahs, creators, or metaphysical forces, but Christianity invites us to believe in a Son and enter into an intimate family relationship with a loving Father. Jesus, the Son of God, came so that we could meet his Father, be adopted into the family of God, and relate to the Almighty God of the universe in an intimate, personal, concrete way as sons and daughters. "God has said of you, 'I will live in you and walk among you, and I will be your God and you shall be my people. . . . I will welcome you, and be a Father to you and you will be my sons and daughters'" (2 Cor. 6:16, 18). If we do not know and relate to God as Father, then we do not really understand the gospel.

Father is the Christian name for God. God is not merely *like* a father as he is like a rock, like a fortress, like a shepherd, or like a warrior. God *is* Father, and he alone defines what true fatherhood means. How tragic, foolish, and arrogant of us to shy away from this name because some human males are poor examples of fatherhood or because our culture regards a God named "Father" as oppressive and patriarchal.

When Jesus was on earth, his whole message was: "Come meet my Dad!" "Look at me," he said, "see what my Dad is like." "See how I imitate him!" "Let me tell you how much my Dad loves me!" "The love I have for you shows you how much my Dad loves you!" "The miracles I do are a result of the compassion and power of my Dad!" "The words I say, the things I teach, are truths from my Dad!" "Listen to me talk to my Dad." "Watch me spend time with my Dad." "Through me, he can be your Dad too!"

Jesus' message appeals to a fundamental need of the human heart: the need to be well fathered. Bringing us into a relationship with our heavenly Father was Christ's ultimate mission and goal. It was the reason he gave his life. Jesus said to him, "I am the way, the truth, and the life. No one comes to the Father except through Me" (John 14:6). We enter into a relationship with Jesus so that he will lead us into the Father's house. At its root, a relationship with the Father is what the gospel is all about.

A number of years ago, in a small town in Spain, there was a young man named Juan. Juan was wild and rebellious. His father's attempts to correct him had failed. At one point Juan stole a large sum of money from his father and ran away from home. Month after month there was no word of him. The father loved his son and longed for him to come home. When he heard that someone had seen Juan in the city, he went to search for him. The father drove up and down the streets, showed Juan's picture to strangers, and checked in bars, but to no avail. Finding his son in such a large city was surely an impossible task.

Finally, an idea struck him. He took out an ad in the local paper. It said: "Juan. All is forgiven. How I long to see you again. Please meet me on Saturday at noon on the steps of city hall. Love, Dad."

When Saturday came and the father went to the appointed place, he found, along with his son, more than a hundred other boys named Juan sitting on the steps of city hall. All the boys were longing, yearning, to have a relationship with the fathers from whom they were estranged.

The human need for being fathered is deep. The longing expressed by these boys is reminiscent of the longing for Father God that resides in each of our hearts. Our spirits long to be fathered by the father of our dreams, our perfect heavenly Father. That's what this book is all about, getting to know God as Father.

We each have a set of thoughts and feelings about God the Father. We automatically believe our assumptions about him are true and seldom stop to consider where we got our concepts. C. S. Lewis tells of a schoolboy who was asked what God was like. "He replied that, as far as he could make out, God was the sort of person who is always snooping around to see if anyone is enjoying himself and then trying to stop it."[3] The boy's perception was distorted. It was based on his experience with his earthly father and not on the clear teachings of Scripture. The task of this book is to help you explore what the Bible says about God the Father, to challenge and correct any misperceptions you might have, and to encourage you to get to know him better. It's my prayer that through these pages you will discover truth, clear away falsehood, experience healing, find hope, and above all, fall deeply in love with the Father who loves you.

In the last verse of the Old Testament, the prophet Malachi looked forward to a time of righteousness when the hearts of the fathers would turn to the children and the hearts of the children to their fathers. Even now, our heavenly Father's heart is turned toward you. Will you turn your heart toward him? Join me In My Father's House, and discover your heart's true home.

Mary

PART 1

The Father Relationship

For you did not receive the spirit of bondage again to fear, but you received the Spirit of adoption by whom we cry out, "Abba, Father." The Spirit Himself bears witness with our spirit that we are children of God.

—ROMANS 8:15–16

You sum up the whole of New Testament teaching in a single phrase, if you speak of it as a revelation of the Fatherhood of the holy Creator. In the same way, you sum up the whole of New Testament religion if you describe it as the knowledge of God as one's holy Father. If you want to judge how well a person understands Christianity, find out how much he makes of the thought of being God's child, and having God as his Father. If this is not the thought that prompts and controls his worship and prayers and his whole outlook on life, it means that he does not understand Christianity very well at all. For everything that Christ taught, everything that makes the New Testament new, and better than the Old, everything that is distinctively Christian as opposed to merely Jewish, is summed up in the knowledge of the Fatherhood of God. "Father" is the Christian name for God.

—J. I. Packer, *Knowing God*

CHAPTER 1

THE FATHERHOOD OF GOD

My Papa was a very tactile kind of dad, wrestling and play-fighting with us when we were small and giving out generous hugs when we were bigger. When I needed to talk, I felt comfortable talking with him. Always, always there was an undercurrent of unconditional love. Even after I was married with a family of my own, the first thing I would do when I went to visit my parents would be to spend a few minutes sitting and talking with my dad in his big recliner, feeling then that all was "right with the world." Because of Dad, it has been an easy transition to grasp the concept of having a personal relationship with a heavenly Father. For me, Father means someone who cares about me, listens to me, protects me, and wants to spend time with me. It means someone who loves me unconditionally and provides an ever-present sense of security. I have been given a glimpse of these things on an intimate level already through my earthly father. How much more wonderful to experience these things to their full potential through getting to know my perfect heavenly Father!

—Kirsten

For although there may be so-called gods, whether in heaven or on earth (as indeed there are many "gods" and many "lords") yet for us there is one God, the Father, from whom are all things and for whom we exist; and one Lord, Jesus Christ, through whom all things came and through whom we exist. (1 Cor. 8:5–6 RSV)

Jesus said to him, "I am the way, the truth, and the life. No one comes to the Father except through Me." (John 14:6)

Whoever denies the Son does not have the Father either; he who acknowledges the Son has the Father also. (1 John 2:23)

And truly our fellowship is with the Father and with His Son Jesus Christ. (1 John 1:3)

God has said of you, "I will live in them and walk among them, and I will be their God and they shall be my people. . . . I will welcome you, and be a Father to you, and you will be my sons and daughters." (2 Cor. 6:16, 18 TLB)

When I was a girl, my favorite day of the week was Sunday. On Sundays we would awaken to the aroma of my Papi's homemade concoction of chocolate porridge topped with meringue and toasted oats. After the bustle of church and entertaining guests for lunch, Papi would take us for a walk in the ravine.

We tossed stones in the brook, raced stick boats, caught frogs, and daredevil balanced across the narrow edge of the tall wooden train trestle. Back home we propped ourselves in front of the old black-and-white television to watch cartoons. Papi would rattle around in the kitchen and eventually appear, carrying newspaper cones piled high with fluffy white popcorn or *purtzeln,* blobs of doughnut-type pastry sprinkled with icing sugar.

The cartoons had barely ended before Papi and Mami whisked us six kids into the station wagon to go to evening church service. There, in the second-to-last pew on the left-hand side of the little pink neighborhood church, I would snuggle in Papi's lap, lean my head on his heart, and fall fast asleep.

For most of us, *father* is not an abstract notion. Like me, you probably have real memories and feelings and thoughts about your father to whom you have, however well or poorly, related. But do you think of God as Father?

Last week I was speaking with a friend who is attending a Christian liberal arts college. When I told her I was writing a study about relating to God as Father, she exclaimed, "What an anachronistic concept!" (An anachronistic idea is one that is unenlightened and out-of-date.) "No one thinks of God as Father anymore," she continued, glancing out the window to check if I had ridden my dinosaur over. "That's positively archaic!"

But is the fatherhood of God an idea that is past its time? Ought we to discard the notion as anachronistic and archaic? Can we relate to God apart from relating to him as Father? The answer, if we take the Bible seriously, is no. If we want to follow the God of the Bible, we must relate to him as Father.

First Corinthians 8:6 tells us that there is only "one God, the Father, from whom all things came and for whom we live" (NIV). Think about this for a moment: There is one God, the Father. And, according to this verse, the Father is the one for whom we live. Many Christians can quote John 14:6 that Jesus is the only way, but we may miss the key phrase. Jesus didn't say, "No one gets to go to heaven without me." He said, "No one comes to the Father." According to Jesus, "coming to the Father" is what Christianity is all about. It's the ultimate goal of salvation.

The importance of knowing God as Father is also taught by the apostle John. John lived to be the oldest and longest-surviving apostle of Jesus. He wrote his Gospel, epistles, and revelation after the other apostles were long dead. I believe God used John's longevity to teach him what was most important. John wrote that if we acknowledge Jesus we also have the Father in our lives (1 John 2:23). He also stressed that "our fellowship is with the Father and with his Son, Jesus Christ" (1 John 1:3 NIV).

If you try to follow the ways of Jesus and the leading of the Holy Spirit, do you realize that when you do this you are ultimately walking in the way of the Father? This is because the Son and the Spirit do not do anything apart from the direction of the Father (John 8:25–26; 12:49; 14:10; 16:13–15).

I have seen many Christians minimize or neglect the importance of working on their relationship with the Father. This is a sad reflection of the times in which we live. Women are told that relating to God as Father is outdated, oppressive, and patriarchal. Men are told that emphasis on God's fatherhood is chauvinistic. As a result, many miss out, for they do not enter into the highest, richest, and most rewarding aspect of their whole relationship with God.

How Did We Get in This Situation?

My friend who seemed to think I rode in with Fred Flintstone reflected a common idea today. Many have given up on the value of fathers. Sadly, our culture has now experienced a couple of generations of poor, misguided, absentee, and often abusive parenting. The state of the home has probably never been poorer in Western civilization. As a result, several things have occurred.

Many children have grown up without a loving relationship with a father. As a result, they carry hurt and bitterness that spills over and poisons other areas of their lives, none more important than the spiritual. The statement that God is Father brings no assurance of love and protection. Rather the idea brings only revulsion.

Try as we might to run from the concept of father, however, God had it hardwired into our souls. When God created people, he made them in the form of a family with a father and a mother. He did so because he knows what we need. Children need to come to trust an earthly dad so they will have the ability to trust the heavenly Father.

Augustine said that our hearts are restless until they find rest in God. In our day we might make a specific elaboration of that truth. Our hearts search for a Father who can heal and protect us. We will never find that Father until we come home to the Father's house.

MORE THAN AN INTELLECTUAL ISSUE

Simply hearing or even superficially believing the truth about God makes little difference in the lives of those who carry a father wound. I have a friend who has spent long years caring for people who have grown up in alcoholic or destructive families. He insists that our early feelings form the foundation of everything we later learn.

If we had a wonderful experience with our earthly father, like Kirsten at the beginning of the chapter, we have a sound foundation on which to build. But when our emotional picture of father is warped, everything that we build on the foundation also becomes twisted. For many, possibly even a majority today, a distorted experience with their earthly father has marred the ultimate experience of both earthly and eternal life.

The need of those who have missed the nurture they deserved has driven me to write this study. I want to walk with you through much that the Bible says about God the Father. I wish that we could sit down together and share these truths heart-to-heart. My prayer is that, wherever you start in this process, you will complete it with a greater appreciation for and experience of the love of your perfect Father God.

The principles we will examine apply to men as well as women. I have boys. I see that they process things differently than women, but they have no less need of a father. The wound for a man who never experienced a father's love may cut differently than for a woman, but it cuts just as deep.

On the other hand, you may be blessed as I have been. You may have experienced the life-affirming and enhancing love of a great father. I believe the Scripture we will examine on these pages will speak to you also. You, too, can grow as we revel in the boundless love of Father God.

How Do You Relate to God?

Consider your relationship with God. Which member of the Trinity do you find yourself most drawn to, the Father, Jesus, or the Holy Spirit? To whom do you most often address your prayers? If you are a Christian, God is your heavenly Father. Consider the implications of this. *Father* means personhood. *Father* means relationship. *Father* means someone we can know and love. Ultimately, when you strip away all the other pictures and elements of God's nature, you come to the fact that he is Father.

We know that God is ultimately Spirit and that he encompasses both masculine and feminine in his character. However, when choosing the best, most accurate word to reveal the essence of his nature and his relationship to us, God chose the word *Father.* God is our good, loving, heavenly Father who wants us to know him on a personal basis.

God is our Father. He is not merely *like* a father, as he is, for example, like a door or rock (John 10:9; Ps. 18:2). Fatherhood is not just an analogy for understanding one aspect of God's character. It is far deeper than that. The term *Father* expresses the essence of who God is and how he relates to us.

God is Father, and he is our Father. He is our Father, and we are his children. This is one of the greatest, most profound truths of the Christian life. The fatherhood of God is the reality Jesus came to reveal and the relationship he came to restore.

Jesus prayed: "O righteous Father! The world has not known You, but I have known You . . . and I have declared to them Your name, and will declare it, that the love with which You loved Me may be in them, and I in them" (John 17:25–26). "This is eternal life, that they may know You" (John 17:3). According to these verses, Jesus introduces (declares) the Father to us so that we might know the Father, experience the love of the Father, and enter into relationship with the Father through his Son, Jesus.

In essence, knowing God the Father is what eternal life is all about.

Knowing God as our Father—as our almighty, loving Father—is the highest, richest, and most rewarding aspect of our whole relationship with him. Knowing God means knowing him as Father. If I do not know God as Father, I do not yet know the meaning of eternal life.

Why do so many people today have such difficulty with the fatherhood of God? Why have I heard so many men and women express fear, anger, or apathy toward the heavenly Father? In the pages ahead we will explore the real-life dimensions of this issue. I pray that the result will be a renewed appreciation for the Father who loves us and a desire to know him.

CHAPTER 2

GOD'S FATHER RELATIONSHIPS

*One of the greatest joys of my life was holding my baby daughter right after
she was born—to realize I had a daughter, to understand that I was a daddy.
What makes it so special to be the daddy of a girl? Maybe it's the way she
calls me Daddy! No one else in the world can call me that. It is also the
incredible way she says it.*

—*Neal*

There is only one God, the Father, of whom are all things, and
we for Him. (1 Cor. 8:6)

But now, O Lord,
You are our Father;
We are the clay, and You our potter;
And all we are the work of Your hand. (Isa. 64:8)

But as many as received Him, to them He gave the right to
become children of God, to those who believe in His name:
who were born, not of blood, nor of the will of the flesh, nor
of the will of man, but of God. (John 1:12–13)

One Saturday night, as I was having coffee with some hockey
moms, waiting for our sons' game to start, we began to discuss the story
of Baby Sarah, a custody case that received much local press attention.
Apparently, a young woman became pregnant in a relationship that
ended shortly after the baby's conception. The father of the child, a
young man in his early twenties, was unaware of the pregnancy.

The woman gave birth and gave the baby girl up for adoption. Shortly thereafter, the young man found out that he had fathered a child and began a court battle against the adoptive parents for custody. After a three-and-a-half-year battle, he appeared to have won. The courts ordered that the adoptive parents return Sarah to her biological father.

The TV footage of the event was heart wrenching. The little girl was sobbing "Daddy" and clinging to her adoptive father, as he, with tears streaming down his face, was giving her to her now-married biological father, who was also crying at the prospect of finally being able to hold his daughter.

As we chatted about this case, most of the women expressed anguish at the thought of separating Sarah from the only mother and father she had ever known. But a few moms questioned how the adoptive parents could ever explain to the child that her biological father had fought long and hard to be allowed to raise her and that they did everything they could to keep the two apart.

This real-life situation is tragic. It begs the question: Who really is Sarah's father? Is it the man who participated in giving her life? Or is it the man who loved, cared for, nurtured, protected, and related to her on a daily basis?

I think we would agree that both he who gave life and he who began to raise this little girl can rightly be called father. We recognize that there are different types of fatherhood. God also is father in different ways. There are four different types of relationships in which the Bible teaches that God is Father.

FATHER OF CREATION

God is Father of all people by virtue of giving them life. Without the Creator Father there would be no life, no existence, and no family of mankind. Paul, when he preached from Mars Hill, quoted the poet Aratus, "For we are also His offspring," to indicate that humans are creatures of God (Acts 17:28). He argued that it is irrational for humans to worship idols they themselves have created. Instead, humans ought to worship the God who created (fathered) them. In Malachi 2:10 the prophet asks, "Have we not all one Father? Has not one God created us?"

FATHER OF ISRAEL

God's second fatherhood relationship is his relationship to his covenant nation, the Jews. The Jewish people, as a whole, were chosen to be children of God: "I will be the God of all the families of Israel, and they shall be My people. . . . For I am a Father to Israel" (Jer. 31:1, 9). Over and over again the children of Israel were challenged to recognize and respond to this family relationship.

"'How gladly would I treat you like sons and give you a desirable land, the most beautiful inheritance of any nation.' I thought you would call me 'Father' and not turn away from following me" (Jer. 3:19 NIV). "If then I am the father, where is My honor?" (Mal. 1:6). God's father relationship with the nation of Israel foreshadowed the time when people from all nations would enter into an adoptive relationship with him.

FATHER OF JESUS

God the Father and God the Son have a unique relationship. Jesus, who exists eternally, is the Father's "only begotten Son" (John 3:16); His "firstborn" (Heb. 1:6). The two relate as Father and Son and yet are equal, both being fully God (Phil. 2:6; Heb. 1:8–9). Although the Jews identified themselves as sons of God, Jesus claimed to be the Son of God in an exclusive manner. He regularly addressed God as "my Father," assuming an intimacy that angered the Jews, for they understood this to mean that Jesus was claiming oneness with God (John 5:17–18).

In more than one hundred references to God as "Father" in the Gospel of John, the overwhelming majority specifically refer to him as the Father of Jesus. The exclusiveness of their relationship is reinforced by the fact that Jesus never coupled himself with others, even his disciples, as being sons of God. He never referred to God as "our" Father, including himself in the "our." Instead, he was careful to differentiate between his own sonship and the sonship of the disciples.

When speaking to Mary, he clearly indicated two distinct relationships: "Go to My brethren and say to them, 'I am ascending to My Father and your Father, and to My God and your God'" (John 20:17).

FATHER OF ADOPTED CHILDREN

The eternal Father-Son relationship between God the Father and Jesus is difficult to understand fully, but the Bible teaches clearly that it is the basis of our own relationship with God. Jesus redeemed us so that we might be adopted into God's family and relate to God as our own Father.

> But when the fullness of time had come, God sent forth His Son, born of a woman, born under the law, to redeem those who were under the law, that we might receive the adoption as sons. And because you are sons, God has sent forth the Spirit of His Son into your hearts, crying out, "Abba, Father!" Therefore you are no longer a slave but a son, and if a son, then an heir of God through Christ. (Gal. 4:4–7)

Adoption, as understood in the Greco-Roman world, was a legal institution whereby one could adopt a child and give that child all the rights and privileges of a naturally born child. It meant a legal change of status from one family identity and inheritance to another.

In the opening verses of Ephesians, Paul explains that God chose us to be adopted into his family (Eph. 1:4–5). It was the Father's choice and the Father's delight to do so. Paul explains that it was according to his "good pleasure." Through Jesus' sacrifice, God legally changes our status so that he is our adoptive Father and we are his children. This is the redemptive relationship with God all believers share.

YOUR ADOPTED FATHER

When you came to Christ, God forgave your sin. But he did more than that. He adopted you. He took you into his house, gave you a new name, a new identity, and a new life. God became your Father, and you became his adopted child.

The cribs of most biological parents are filled easily. They decide to have a child, and a child comes. In fact, sometimes a child comes even when the parents do not plan or expect one. But have you ever heard of an unplanned adoption?

Couples who have been unable to have biological children and who choose to adopt know what it is to long for a child. They know what it is to yearn to share their love. They know what it means to search and to wait. Their desire to love is so strong that they will take a child with a blemished past and a dubious future.

This is just what the Father does. He rescues orphans from despair and brings them into the warmth of his family. He planned for you, looked for you, found you, signed the papers, and brought you home.

Galatians 4:4–5 is both a favorite Scripture of mine and a concise summary of redemption. Paul wrote: "But when the time had fully come, God sent his Son, born of a woman, born under law, to redeem those under law, that we might receive the full rights of sons" (NIV).

Why did God adopt you? Was it because you were beautiful, smart, or talented? Read the following paraphrase of Ephesians 1:4–5 from the *Living Bible*:

> Long ago, even before he made the world, God chose us to be his very own, through what Christ would do for us; he decided then to make us holy in his eyes, without a single fault—we who stand before him covered with his love. His unchanging plan has always been to adopt us into his own family by sending Jesus Christ to die for us. And he did this because he wanted to! (Eph. 1:4–5 TLB)

My husband, Brent, could barely wait for our first child to be born. Every night he would caress my expanding belly and talk to the baby he could not yet see. Finally the time arrived! Our son was born, and the nurse gently placed the warm, wrinkly bundle of flesh into his father's waiting arms. Brent was overcome with inexpressible emotion: love, joy, tenderness, pride. He was a father! Your heavenly Father chose you as his child before the foundation of the world. He did this because "he wanted to." This choice gave him much joy and pleasure (Eph. 1:4–6). Consider your Father God anticipating the time when you would be born again. The love, joy, tenderness, and pride of almighty God, your heavenly Father, was focused on you, his new adopted son or daughter.

Do you delight in having God as your Father as much as he delights in having you as his child? Wouldn't it be a good time to pray and acknowledge God as your Father? Thank him for choosing you to be his child.

CHAPTER 3
LIKE FATHER, LIKE SON

If my father's car was in the driveway when I got home from school, I knew the evening would go relatively well. He could be sullen and moody, but an early arrival indicated that he would not be drunk. No car meant that he had gone to the bar with the guys from work. As supper came and went, I could see the apprehension in Mama's face grow. She would send me to my room long before bedtime just so I wouldn't witness his homecoming.

But though I did not always see it, I always heard. He was loud. He was angry. He swore. He smashed things, threw things, and sometimes even turned on Mama. I would hide in my closet or under the bedcovers, trying to shut out the sound.

Once, when I heard Mama cry, I ran from my room and tried to pull him away, begging him not to hurt her. But he was too strong. He threw me against the floor, pinned me down, and warned me never to come between him and Mama again. I'll never forget the weight of his body, the wild look in his glazed eyes, or the smell of his hot, liquor-laden breath. I was so afraid.

Somehow we all managed to survive those years. But I never really trusted my father. And after I became a Christian, I felt the same way about God the Father. I could relate to Jesus—the gentle, kind healer who gave his life for me—but not to his Father, whom I perceived to be angry, judgmental, and callused.

Over the past few years, my perceptions about God the Father have slowly begun to change. I am beginning to believe what Jesus said about his Father instead of relying on my experience with my earthly father.

—*Julie*

The Son is the radiance of God's glory and the exact representation of his being. (Heb. 1:3 NIV)

Jesus said to him, "Have I been with you so long, and yet you
have not known Me, Philip? He who has seen Me has seen the
Father; so how can you say, 'Show us the Father'?"
(John 14:9)

Jesus gave them this answer: "I tell you the truth, the Son can
do nothing by himself; he can do only what he sees his Father
doing, because whatever the Father does the Son also does.
For the Father loves the Son and shows him all he does."
(John 5:19–20 NIV)

Righteous Father, though the world does not know you,
I know you, and they know that you have sent me. I have
made you known to them, and will continue to make you
known in order that the love you have for me may be in them
and that I myself may be in them. (John 17:25–26 NIV)

In my Father's house are many rooms; if it were not so,
I would have told you . . . You know the way to the place where
I am going . . . I am the way and the truth and the life. No one
comes to the Father except through me. (John 14:2, 4, 6 NIV)

Lance, a Christian friend of mine, recently went on a search for
his birth father who had walked out on him and his mother thirty
years ago. Lance had had no contact with his father since he was a toddler and remembered little about him. After a few months of searching, Lance located his father and went to see him. "It was uncanny,"
he related, "like looking in a mirror! I look like him. We have the same
likes and dislikes. We even have the same mannerisms!"

I don't know why he was so surprised. It was his father, after all.
One would expect that there would be at least a bit of resemblance.

We constantly compare children to parents and extended family
to determine who in the family they resemble. "She's got her father's
eyes." "She's got her momma's hair." "She's got a temper like her
grandpa!" "She's got her grandma's love for music."

What the parents and grandparents are like gives an indication of the features that we might see in the child. "Like mother, like daughter," or "like father, like son," go the sayings.

Sometimes, like Lance and his father, a child resembles one parent so strongly that one wonders if only that parent's genes were passed on to the child. The child seems more like a carbon copy than a unique creation.

JESUS LOOKS EXACTLY LIKE HIS FATHER

The Bible tells us that Jesus looks just like his Father. He is the spitting image of Father God (2 Cor. 4:4). The semblance is so strong that he is said to be "the exact representation of his being" (Heb. 1:3 NIV). A carbon-copy likeness. Like Father, like Son.

No human has seen the Father (John 5:37; 6:46). But because Jesus is the exact image of the Father, we can know what the Father is like by looking at Jesus.

In John 14:9 (NIV) Jesus said to Philip: "Don't you know me, Philip, even after I have been among you such a long time? Anyone who has seen me has seen the Father. How can you say, 'Show us the Father'?" Jesus informed Philip that because he had seen Jesus, Philip had also seen the Father.

JESUS HAS THE SAME PERSONALITY AS HIS FATHER

Jesus has the same personality as his Father. He possesses all of the same attributes. The Father is holy, and so is Jesus. The Father is faithful and just, and so is Jesus. The Father is merciful, and so is Jesus.

Look at this list of some of the traits we can observe in Jesus. Think about how many of the traits reflect what the Father is like.

- He has a great love for people. (John 15:9)
- He is gentle. (Matt. 11:29)
- He cares for and looks after his friends. (John 10:11–18)
- He is deeply moved by the suffering of his friends. (John 11:33)
- He is moved with compassion for the lost. (Matt. 9:36)
- He uses his strength to serve. (Matt. 20:28)
- He is patient. (1 Tim. 1:16)
- He forgives sins. (Luke 7:48)

- He is fair. He judges unbelief and those who reject truth. (Matt. 11:20–24)
- He has a high regard for women. (Luke 13:16)

How many of the traits did you think reflect Father God's personality as well as Jesus' personality. I'll give you a hint. They all do. Everything that you notice about Jesus' personality is a part of the personality of his Father. The Father is not different from his Son. He is the same. Like Son, like Father. Look back over the list. Do any of the characteristics of the Father surprise you? Do they go against what you thought the Father was like?

JESUS DOES WHAT HIS FATHER DOES

In Bible times most sons grew up in the trade and profession of their fathers. Because Mary's husband, Joseph, was a carpenter, Jesus learned to be a carpenter too. Joseph taught Jesus how to use the tools. Jesus copied Joseph's example.

But when the time came, Jesus left the profession of his adopted earthly father, Joseph, and took on the profession of his birth Father, God. Jesus did everything according to the way he saw his Father God do it. Here, too, Jesus copied his Father's example.

I'll never forget the moment John 5:19–20 (NIV) powerfully struck me. It seemed at that moment as if the phrase "whatever the Father does the Son also does" jumped off of the page. Let me try to show you what I mean. In this Scripture those who rejected Jesus were trying to kill him because he was breaking their understanding of the Sabbath law and claiming that God was his Father. Here is the passage:

> Jesus gave them this answer: "I tell you the truth, the Son can do nothing by himself; he can do only what he sees his Father doing, because whatever the Father does the Son also does. For the Father loves the Son and shows him all he does. Yes, to your amazement he will show him even greater things than these." (John 5:19–20 NIV)

Everything Jesus did when he was on earth was either something he saw the Father do or something he was directed by the Father to do. Jesus did nothing apart from the example and the directive of his Father:

- As the Father loved Jesus, so Jesus loves us. (John 15:9)
- As the Father has life in himself, so Jesus has life in himself. (John 5:26)
- As the Father sent Jesus, so Jesus sends his disciples. (John 20:21)
- As the Father does miracles, so Jesus does miracles. (John 10:25, 38)
- As the Father continually works on our behalf, so Jesus works on our behalf. (John 5:16–17)
- As the Father does good works, so Jesus does good works. (John 10:32)

Jesus questioned the Jews who wanted to stone him, "Why then do you accuse me of blasphemy because I said, 'I am God's Son'? Do not believe me unless I do what my Father does" (John 10:36–37 NIV).

Jesus argued that his works proved that he was the Son of God. People should have seen the family likeness, for he acted just like his Father. Jesus was trained in his Father's profession.

JESUS KNOWS HIS FATHER INTIMATELY

Jesus said, "The Father knows me and I know the Father" (John 10:15 NIV). The word *know* indicates an intimate and personal relation between the person knowing and the one who is known. In the Old Testament, if a man *knew* his wife, it meant that he had intimate relations with her.

The relationship between Father and Son goes beyond that of friends. It is far deeper. It is even deeper than the most intimate of human relationships between a husband and wife. The Father and Son are so intimate that it is difficult to find words to adequately express the extent of their relationship. Jesus described it this way: "Father, . . . we are one" (John 21–22 NIV). "You are in me and I am in you" (John 17:21 NIV; also see 10:38).

John 17:25–26 tells us that Jesus, the Son of God, is the only one who really knows the Father. We can only get to know the Father through getting to know the one who really knows him. Read for yourself these words from Jesus' high priestly prayer:

> Righteous Father, though the world does not know you,
> I know you, and they know that you have sent me. I have

made you known to them, and will continue to make you known in order that the love you have for me may be in them and that I myself may be in them. (John 17:25–26 NIV)

Consider what we've examined in this chapter. As the image of the invisible God, Jesus looks exactly like His Father. Christ has the same personality as his Father. He does what his Father does, and he loves his Father intimately. But the Bible tells us even more about this relationship.

JESUS IS THE WAY TO THE FATHER'S HOUSE

The first few verses of John 14 contain some of the most often quoted words of Jesus. The occasion was the night before the crucifixion. For months Jesus had been telling his thick-headed disciples that he was going to Jerusalem to die. Finally the message began to soak in. On the eve of his own suffering, Jesus comforted his friends:

"Do not let your hearts be troubled. Trust in God; trust also in me. In my Father's house are many rooms; if it were not so, I would have told you. I am going there to prepare a place for you. And if I go and prepare a place for you, I will come back and take you to be with me that you also may be where I am. You know the way to the place where I am going."

Thomas said to him, "Lord, we don't know where you are going, so how can we know the way?"

Jesus answered, "I am the way and the truth and the life. No one comes to the Father except through me." (John 14:1–6 NIV)

The Father sent his Son to bring us into the Father's house. In the future we will go there and see him face-to-face. But we do not have to wait to begin to enjoy this privilege. We can begin to enjoy the Father's house the moment we meet Jesus. We will not fully experience it until we reach heaven, but even now we can know that we have passed through the door.

Let me say something that ought to shock you a bit. We need to realize that knowing Jesus is not the ultimate goal of Christianity. God's purpose has always been that we know the Father through Jesus.

Coming into the Father's house through his Son is what the Christian journey is all about. We come to Jesus so that we can get to know our heavenly Father.

In the following verses note who initiates the invitation for you to come to the Father's house:

> "All that the Father gives me will come to me, and whoever comes to me I will never drive away." (John 6:37 NIV)

> "No one can come to me unless the Father who sent me draws him, and I will raise him up at the last day. It is written in the Prophets: 'They will all be taught by God.' Everyone who listens to the Father and learns from him comes to me." (John 6:44–45 NIV)

> Praise be to the God and Father of our Lord Jesus Christ, who has blessed us in the heavenly realms with every spiritual blessing in Christ. For he chose us in him before the creation of the world to be holy and blameless in his sight. (Eph. 1:3–4 NIV)

The Father gave the invitation for you to come to his house! He sent his Son to make it possible for you to come. You have entered the door of his house through Jesus. But are you content to stay just inside the door? Or do you long to travel further in to get to know its owner, your Father?

Which of the following two statements do you want to describe how you feel about being in the Father's house?

- Jesus brings me to his Father's house, but I pay no attention to the Father.
- Jesus brings me to his Father's house, and I am falling in love with the Father.

If you are attracted to Jesus, you will really love the Father! That's because Jesus reveals the Father to us. The fatherhood of God is the reality that Jesus came to reveal and the relationship he came to restore. Close this chapter by thanking the Father that he brought you to his house through his Son, Jesus. Tell the Father that you would like to move further into his house to get to know him better.

CHAPTER 4

DAUGHTERS AS SONS OF GOD

My dad died when I was two years old. Growing up without an earthly father has left in me a deep ache, a lonely gap, a hunger. The longing to be held and be loved and to know my father is ever present. I get choked up when I watch little girls run and throw themselves confidently into the big, strong embraces of their fathers, laughing and squealing, "Daddy! Pick me up!" or "Daddy's home!" or just plain "Daddy!" I regard the father-daughter relationship as the most vulnerable, and thus the most tender of all human relationships. It blows my mind when I think that God longs to relate to me in that way.

—Patti

> For you are all sons of God through faith in Christ Jesus. For as many of you as were baptized into Christ have put on Christ. There is neither Jew nor Greek, there is neither slave nor free, there is neither male nor female; for you are all one in Christ Jesus. . . . And because you are sons, God has sent forth the Spirit of His Son into your hearts, crying out, "Abba, Father!" (Gal. 3:26–28; 4:6)

Ko Myung-ok glanced nervously at the ultrasound screen, praying she would be spared a fifth abortion. Her heart leaped when the technician showed her what she wanted to see: It was a boy; she could carry the fetus to term. "Finally, it was a son," she recounted. "I felt as if I had plucked a star from the sky."

Other women appearing with her on the morning talk show nodded their heads sympathetically. There is a strong traditional preference for sons in South Korea. In one year alone, thirty thousand

27

female children were aborted because their parents did not want a daughter.

SONS OR DAUGHTERS

When I was in university, I met a beautiful young woman named Sondra who was drawn to the gospel yet was resisting becoming a Christian because she thought God the Father was prejudiced against women. This is not an uncommon thought. In fact, it has become increasingly common in recent decades.

Contemporary women have been taught that men are, by nature, abusive and oppressive, and that their prejudice against women is apparent, if not centered, in the Christian religion. I clearly remember a philosophy class in which I heard that the Christian God was unacceptable to women because he identified himself with masculine pronouns and with the name Father. Such a God, the professor reasoned, legitimized male dominance and abuse of women. In her mind such a God did not want daughters.

Is it true? Is Father God partial to sons? Look at what the following verses say about the issue:

- Romans 8:14—For as many as are led by the Spirit of God, these are sons of God.
- Romans 8:19—Creation eagerly waits for the revealing of the sons of God.
- Galatians 3:26—For you are all sons of God through faith in Christ Jesus.
- Hebrews 2:10—He brings many sons to glory.

If you looked up these verses in an accurate translation of the Bible, you would find the word *sons* in every instance. Now before you dismiss this as a cultural or literary idiosyncrasy, or before you make the assumption that God does not like women, let us take a closer look at what is meant by the word *sons*.

In the Hebrew language, the word *son* can be used figuratively to characterize a person's origin and nature. Hence, in the Old Testament, we see "son of death" (1 Sam. 20:31) and "sons of captivity" (Ezra 4:1).

In the New Testament, we see such expressions as "sons of the prophets" (Acts 3:25), "sons of wisdom" (Matt. 11:19), "sons of the resurrection" (Luke 20:36), "son of peace" (Luke 10:6), "son of the devil"

(Acts 13:10), and "sons of disobedience" (Eph. 2:2). Thus, when the term "sons of men" is used in the Bible, it means humans, but it also denotes that these people are of mortal origin and character.

Understanding this meaning of the word *son* helps us understand why the Jews found it so offensive that Jesus called himself the son of God. In essence, they understood Jesus to be claiming that he originated with God and that he was of the same character as God. That is why the Jews persecuted Jesus and sought to kill him (John 5:18–23).

Understanding *son* in this way also helps clarify what is meant when the term "sons of God" is used of humans. *Son* in this context does not mean "male offspring." It refers to a person who has originated from God and has the same nature or character of God.

This is an astounding concept. In calling believers his sons, God is communicating that believers find their origin in him and that they bear the same characteristics he does. Furthermore, it strongly correlates a person's redemptive relationship to the Father with Jesus' relationship to the Father. Jesus is the Son of God; and believers, as sons of God, enter into a similarly intimate family relationship with the Father.

BECOMING A SON OF GOD

But who can be a "son of God"? Is it a privilege reserved for males? Read the following passage that describes the prerequisite for being a son of God.

> For you are all sons of God through faith in Christ Jesus. For as many of you as were baptized into Christ have put on Christ. There is neither Jew nor Greek, there is neither slave nor free, there is neither male nor female; for you are all one in Christ Jesus. . . . And because you are sons, God has sent forth the Spirit of His Son into your hearts, crying out, "Abba, Father!" (Gal. 3:26–28; 4:6)

According to this passage, it makes no difference whether you are Jew or Gentile, slave or free, male or female. Think about this verse again. Condensed, it says, "You are all sons. There is neither male nor female."

Paul is explaining that being a son of God has nothing to do with being male or female. Figuratively, a believing woman is just as much a son of God as a believing man.

If you go back to the passages in Romans, Galatians, and Hebrews, you can try another exercise. You can look the word *sons* up in a Greek Bible dictionary. Here is one such result. Read carefully: "Child (of either gender), descendant (in any generation); by extension: a term of endearment; one of a class or kind, for example, a 'son of the resurrection' is one who participates in the resurrection. 'The Son of Man' is an OT phrase usually meaning 'human being,' that in the NT is used almost exclusively as a messianic title (see Dan. 7:13), emphasizing Jesus' humanity" (Accordance Bible software).

Sounds like my Greek computer software said the same thing I'd concluded from the other study of Scripture. In this context *son* has nothing to do with gender. It has everything to do with relationship. If you have recognized your sin and turned to Christ, you are a son of God. The term links and identifies you with Jesus, the Son of God. The term "son of God" refers to your origin and character, not your gender.

The term "sons of God" includes women. Lest there be any uncertainty that women are included, most Bible authors who identify believers as "sons of God" also incorporate the more generic term *child* into the discussion.

In Romans 8:23, Paul refers to his audience as "sons" (NIV). Just a few verses earlier, he refers to them as "children" (v. 17). In Hebrews 2:10, believers are called "sons"; in verse 14 they are called "children." God himself is careful to specify that he is Father equally to both men and women: "I will be a Father to you, And you shall be My sons and daughters, Says the LORD Almighty" (2 Cor. 6:18).

This point is so critical for you to embrace that I am not above a little overkill. The following verses speak of the adoptive relationship believers have with Father God. Not one of these verses uses the term *son*. Instead each uses the term *child*.

> Yet to all who received him, to those who believed in his
> name, he gave the right to become children of God.
> (John 1:12 NIV)

So that you may become blameless and pure, children of God without fault in a crooked and depraved generation, in which you shine like stars in the universe. (Phil. 2:15 NIV)

How great is the love the Father has lavished on us, that we should be called children of God! And that is what we are! The reason the world does not know us is that it did not know him. (1 John 3:1 NIV)

And again, "I will put my trust in him." And again he says, "Here am I, and the children God has given me." (Heb. 2:13 NIV)

The sons of God are Jews, Greeks, and Gentiles; black and white; despised and respected; rich and poor; tall and short; men and women. All the features that externally define us are inconsequential when it comes to salvation, for Jesus brings "many sons to glory" (Heb. 2:10).

THE BEAUTY OF GENDER IMAGERY

In our day few people of either sex appreciate the depth and beauty of gender symbolism. We are taught, instead, to resent it. But this symbolism reveals the nature of God's character and the nature of his relationship to us.

God uses male pronouns not because he is male but because the symbolism most accurately represents his essence, who he is in relationship with the other members of the divine nature and who he is in relationship to humankind.

God is Father. Jesus is Son. Father-Son is how the two relate. This imagery is extended to the Father's relationship with us. Redeemed women, along with men, are figuratively "sons of God." We relate to the first person of the Trinity as a child relates to a father.

Using other gender imagery, the Bible teaches that redeemed men, together with women are "the bride of Christ." Christ has a husband-wife relationship with his church (see Eph. 5). Many find gender imagery discriminatory, and some translators have even begun to gloss it over or rewrite it out of the Bible. This trend is tragic. Not only do we insult God by changing his self-revealed designation, but we also lose sight of deep, profound, beautiful object lessons. God has made us male and female. This fact is not trivial or unimportant. On the contrary, it's vitally important that we honor God's design for male and female. The male-female relationship was meant to mirror deep, profound truths about the nature and character of God.

The Bible uses gender imagery for a reason. That reason is not, as some have argued, that God favors one sex over the other. God does not refer to men as "bride" because he values women more than men. Nor does he call women "sons" because he values males more than females. No, he calls men "bride" to teach of the love, intimacy, and oneness of Christ's relationship to the church. He calls women "sons" because we are included by grace in the same category as his only Son, Jesus. Jesus is God's begotten Son; I am God's adopted son.

If we think the symbolism has something to do with which sex is better than the other, we are totally missing the point. This symbolism has little to do with us and everything to do with God. And far from being exclusive, we would be hard-pressed to find symbols that include women in God's agenda to a greater extent than the ones he has revealed. The gender imagery of the Bible is beautiful. It ought to be embraced, not neutered.

How comfortable do you feel when you read Bible passages using gender imagery? Is the way you feel shaped by the world or by God's Spirit? Do you believe God loves sons more than daughters?

Sondra, whom I introduced to you earlier in the chapter, did take the risk of faith and put her trust in God. I watched her struggle with gender and God issues for many years. But gradually Sondra came to trust God fully as her loving Father. She found peace and blessing in the biblical imagery and in who God made her to be as a woman.

God values women. And to him Sondra is like a shining star plucked out of the sky. You also are his shining star. If you are his girl, he loves and values you just as much as he values his boys.

If you are a woman who struggles with this issue, I encourage you to talk honestly with the Father about it. Acknowledge the truth of Scripture to him, namely that he values you as a woman. If you are a man, I thank you for taking this journey with us and for being sensitive to this struggle many women in our culture share.

I sincerely hope this chapter has clearly presented several truths.
1. In the Bible the word *son* is often used to characterize a person's origin and nature.
2. With regards to salvation, women are also sons of God.

3. Gender imagery is used in the Bible to teach us truths about God. It does not indicate that God plays favorites or that he regards one sex as better than the other.

4. God the Father loves his children, so much so, that he sacrificed his only begotten Son in order to bring "many sons to glory" (Heb. 2:10).

CHAPTER 5

THE INFLUENCE OF EARTHLY FATHERS

When I think about my two fathers, earthly and heavenly, the picture that comes to mind is that of a warped, smudged window. God is on the other side of this window. My dad is the window. I see God through the warped window of my dad so that the image I have of God the Father is really warped. Emotionally, I fear ridicule. I fear not meeting up to his expectations. I fear closeness and intimacy. But God has revealed to me through his Word that my heavenly Father is not anything like Dad. I have begun to pray that God would give me the strength to move the window of my earthly dad aside so I can see my heavenly Father clearly for who he is.

—Lisa

> For you did not receive the spirit of bondage again to fear, but
> you received the Spirit of adoption by whom we cry out,
> "Abba, Father." The Spirit Himself bears witness with our
> spirit that we are children of God. (Rom. 8:15–16)

An ancient creed of the church begins with the affirmation: "We believe in One God, the Father Almighty, Creator and Maker of all things; from whom all fatherhood in heaven and on earth is named. This part of the creed is based on a passage in Ephesians in which Paul prays to the Father of our Lord Jesus Christ, from whom all fatherhood in heaven and earth is named" (Eph. 3:14–15). Evidently the early church regarded this as an essential statement about the nature of God. These verses contain two basic thoughts: (1) The first person of the Trinity is identified as the Father of Jesus, and (2) all earthly fatherhood is named after him.

The word *fatherhood* (Gr. *patria*), often translated "family," signifies the historical origin of a household from its patriarch. It refers to a family of people that are related to each other through descent from a common father. The basic thrust of this passage, therefore, is that the fatherhood of God stands behind the whole scheme of ordered family relationships. Let me say that again: The fatherhood of God stands behind the whole scheme of ordered family relationships.

This is an extremely significant thought. It means that God has patterned earthly fatherhood and family relationships after his own fatherhood. It means that God, not man, defines the content of true fatherhood. It also means that a natural link or association connects earthly fatherhood and the fatherhood of God. Our experience with our earthly fathers can and will affect our perception of God.

The association between earthly fathers and Father God was taught by Jesus. He reasoned that if earthly fathers, who are evil, know how to act with kindness and generosity toward their children, how much more does the heavenly Father know how to do so? (Matt. 7:9–10; Luke 11:13; see also Heb. 12:9–11). Jesus taught that earthly fatherhood, despite its sinfulness, points to the perfect fatherhood of God.

Earthly fathers paint pictures of fatherhood for us. If I were to pose in front of a large group of people and ask them to draw a portrait of me, I would receive a wide variety of results. From someone with no artistic skill or little patience, the portrait might only resemble me in that it also has two eyes, a nose, and a mouth. If the portrait were drawn by a child, it might be totally unrecognizable as human. If there were an artist in the crowd, who took the time to look at me and carefully study my features, the portrait would be highly representative of the way I look. But even the best portrait would fall short. A two-dimensional portrait is inadequate to accurately represent a three-dimensional being.

It is the same way with earthly fathers. Some men sketch fairly good pictures of true fatherhood; some sketch a poor representation. Some portraits are covered with black scribbles, the image barely recognizable. It is natural that we look to our earthly fathers to image fatherhood for us. Their fatherhood is seen and experienced directly. But the image they draw is, at best, only two-dimensional. It is only an image, not the real thing. The fatherhood of our earthly fathers is merely a shadow of the true fatherhood of God.

To develop our relationship with God the Father, we need to recognize the source of the image of fatherhood that we carry in our hearts. Did our perception of fatherhood come primarily from the portrait of our earthly father, or has it come from the portrait of the perfect fatherhood of God as revealed in the Bible and by the Holy Spirit?

Please allow me to ask you a series of questions about the portrait you received from your earthly father. These questions may be cause for rejoicing if you had a positive experience with your father, or they may be uncomfortable for you to consider. I am asking them to expose where you are getting your ideas about fatherhood. Even if these questions bring pain, they will help you separate the portrait from the real thing. They will help you identify areas in which you may require healing or correction in your thoughts about fatherhood, and open the door toward a deeper relationship with Father God.

PRESENT OR ABSENT?

Was your earthly father more often absent or present for you? Many have experienced fathers who were not physically present because of long work hours, travel, divorce, or death. Others had fathers who were physically present but emotionally absent. Emotional absence can result from several situations. Many fathers grew up with absentee fathers themselves, so they simply lack the skills to relate to their children. Addiction to substances, rage, work, or a hundred other behaviors have rendered many fathers emotionally absent.

Since a child's world is all the child knows, the reason for a parent's emotional absence is less important than the simple recognition of the fact. If we grew up with a father who was absent, may we have hung that same portrait in God's place?

LOVING OR UNLOVING?

Would you characterize your father as loving or unloving? Did he show you that he cared for you? Did he affirm you, or did you feel you could not please him?

One of the saddest parts of J. R. R. Tolkien's *Lord of the Rings* trilogy is the relationship between Denathor, the steward of Minas Tirith, and his son, Faramir. Faramir is a captain in the army of Gondor. He is a good, brave, wise young man. The men under his command respect him. But the relationship between Faramir and his father is strained. Faramir is the second-born son. Denathor adores Faramir's older brother—loves, affirms, and recognizes him—but constantly belittles, shuns, and criticizes his younger son. As the story unfolds, it becomes clear that Faramir's heart is filled with pain and longing. His deepest ambition is to win his father's love and respect. Though he does his best, obeys his father, and puts his life on the line for his country time and again, his efforts never seem good enough. Denathor remains unloving toward him. In one poignant moment, as Faramir obeys his father's rash command and rides out to certain defeat and death, he hears a friend call out, "Faramir, your father loves you, and he will remember it before the end." Faramir never experienced the love of his father, even though, as Faramir's friend predicted, Denathor remembered just how much he loved his son in the end.

Contrast this image with a picture I once clipped from a newspaper. The picture is of a house with a broken front window. Dark streaks of blood below the broken window vividly stain the house's white siding. The accompanying story tells of a father who sliced his hands to ribbons and severely gashed his body as he desperately broke his way through glass to rescue his children from a fire. The image is powerful. It speaks volumes of how much that father loved his children.

What about you? Does your heart ache for the love of your earthly father? How well did he express his love? Did you feel secure that he loved you, or were you left guessing as to the extent of his love? How has your earthly father's love impacted your perception of the love of your heavenly Father?

Affirming or Nonaffirming

Did your earthly father tell you that you were valuable? I am convinced that every human hungers and thirsts for affirmation. It encourages us to be more than we thought we could. Without it we often wither and die. Of all the ways to show love, none exceed the importance of affirmation.

Affirmation does not mean we approve of everything another person does. In fact, the best affirmation separates person from performance. It says you are important; I value you; whether you fail or succeed, I'm proud of you.

Males grow up in a competitive culture. Many feel that the only way to achieve worth is to be faster, stronger, or better than others. They push each other, and many confuse that pressure for caring: the best coach yells the loudest. Couple the pressure to perform with the fact that many fathers never experienced parenting by their own dads. Unfortunately, the net result is often stoic, silent fathers who neither see the need nor have the skills to affirm their children. They often ignore daughters and drive sons. At the funeral of such a father, you may hear a son or daughter say, "I know my dad loved me." But the speaker may be at a loss to give any evidence of the fact.

If your father fits any of this description, what would you give to have him put his arms around you and tell you how important you are to him? If a huge lump grows in your throat at that thought, you know what I mean. If tears fill your eyes, how much have your feelings for your dad shaped your expectations from God?

I'm convinced that many people feel that God maintains a consistent attitude of indifference, if not anger, toward them. The last thing they can believe is that God affirms, validates, or applauds them. In contrast to this pervasive expectation, Scripture tells us of the God who "will take great delight in you, he will quiet you with his love, he will rejoice over you with singing" (Zeph. 3:17 NIV).

HUMBLE OR PROUD

Humility does not mean weakness. In fact, the opposite is true. It takes a strong man or woman to be humble because humility looks honestly at our own humanity. Pride, on the other hand, appears strong but is weak. Pride is self-centered. Humility can focus on others' needs. Pride makes every situation about self. Humility realizes that God is the center, so the humble person can step aside and enjoy the accomplishments of others. Was your father characterized by humility or pride? Was he self-serving or self-giving? Did everything that happened in your home center around him? Was he self-centered and attention-seeking? How has that affected your life and your perception of God the Father?

PATIENT OR QUICK-TEMPERED

Dale described an incident on the farm where he grew up. His dad let him drive the tractor. There were deep furrows, and his dad knew the wheels would naturally follow the straight ruts. But the boy wanted to steer the tractor, and forcefully turned the wheel. Soon the tractor was running amok, directly across the plowed field, making a mess of a day's hard work. When the father finally caught the tractor and got it shut down, the young boy knew he was in trouble. His dad paused a moment, then said: "Well, I guess we're gonna have to fire you as a tractor driver and hire you as a pickup driver." Like Jesus recommissioning Peter after his denial (John 21), Dale's father took a vulnerable moment and affirmed his son.

Think of a time when you really blew it as a child. It could have been childish irresponsibility, a spilling-your-milk moment. Or it could be something more serious. How did your father respond? Or how do you imagine your father responding if he wasn't around? Was he patient or quick-tempered? Was he gentle with you or harsh? Would you describe him as kind or cruel? How much do each of those responses carry over to what you feel about Father God?

FOUNDATIONAL IMAGES

There are many other traits and characteristics of your earthly father that could mask your perception of God the Father. Was your father insecure or confident? Was he controlling, or did he concentrate on empowering his children? Could you count on him, or was he undependable? Did he provide for the family, or did you worry about basic needs? Was he stingy or generous?

Don't misunderstand. The purpose here is not to blame good old dad. This journey isn't about him. It's about what lies buried in our own hearts. The point is to evaluate honestly how your relationship with your father has shaped your feelings and attitudes toward God and toward life. Was your father:

- Praise-giving or critical
- Affectionate or cold
- Intimate or superficial
- Good listener or poor listener
- Permissive or strict

- Willing to serve others or demanding of service
- Strong or weak
- Communicative or noncommunicative
- Flexible or rigid
- Encouraging or discouraging
- Honest or deceptive
- Responsible or irresponsible
- Happy or unhappy
- Nonprotective or overly protective
- Approachable or unapproachable
- Gentle or abusive
- Keeps promises or breaks promises
- Consistent or inconsistent
- Fair or unfair
- Forgiving or unforgiving
- Accepting or rejecting
- Attentive or neglectful
- Involved or uninvolved
- Initiatory or passive
- Hard worker or lazy

In the above list what traits have had the greatest positive impact on your perception of fatherhood? Look through the list again and identify the trait or traits that have had the greatest negative impact on your perception of fatherhood. Do you regard these positive fatherhood traits as being part of the fatherhood of God? Emotionally, do you fear that these negative fatherhood traits are also part of Father God's character?

Our emotional picture of father is anchored in the deepest part of our being. Whether we learned that father protects us and can be trusted or we learned that father is absent or abusive, that image stays buried as the foundation of our later relationships.

We come along later and build all sorts of ideas and attitudes on the foundation. However, unless we dig deeply into our own hearts, that original foundation stays unchanged. As a result, many people feel like two opposite forces tear at their souls. They may believe in their heads that God is good, loving, and powerful. But in their emotions they fear that God is actually harsh, abusive, or likely to abandon them.

My friend Dianne did the difficult work of examining her legacy. She honestly declared:

> I have a tremendous fear of God the Father. I fear being abandoned, rejected. . . . I don't feel as though I can trust God. My father had a violent, raging anger inside. This resulted in bursts of swearing and beatings of our mother, and sometimes us children. I am totally afraid of God my Father as well as my earthly father. I felt I was never good enough. My sisters and I were victims of incest, which resulted in feelings of betrayal, abandonment, rejection, and no trust in God the Father. I am still searching for significance in who I am in Christ as God's beloved child.

My heart goes out to Dianne and all the women and men like her. You may be scared, you may not trust God, and you may be holding back, but Father God loves you and wants you to know and experience true fatherhood. He has promised that the Holy Spirit will replace your fear and draw you toward the Father's heart with the gentle touch of his love. For when you gave your heart to Jesus, you did not receive the spirit of bondage to fear, but you received the Spirit of adoption by whom you are enabled to cry out, "Abba, Father" (Rom. 8:15).

If you have a fear of God the Father, cry out, "Abba, Father," in prayer to him. Ask the Holy Spirit to free you from the bondage of fear. Ask him to help you be vulnerable enough to look past the image of fatherhood you have experienced—however good or bad that may have been—into the eyes of your true, perfect, loving heavenly Father.

CHAPTER 6

LONGING FOR THE FATHER

My relationship with my dad is an extension of my relationship with God the Father. I enjoy being with my dad a lot. Dad loves life. He is affectionate. He gives and wants affection. He is generous. And with my dad, I always felt safe, supported, and provided for. But the first thing that comes to mind when I consider my dad is that he, more than anyone else, has played a visionary role in my life. He has always challenged me to think big, to invest my life wisely, and to change my world. I know without a doubt that my dad loves me, believes in me, and wants the best for me. This has made it easy for me to accept God as Father. In fact, "Father" is the primary way I relate to God. Based on my relationship with my dad, I have no problems giving God the Father my obedience and trust. I think I would be miles behind in Christianity had it not been for a strong relationship with my dad.

—Karen

> For you did not receive the spirit of bondage again to fear, but you received the Spirit of adoption by whom we cry out, "Abba, Father." The Spirit Himself bears witness with our spirit that we are children of God. (Rom. 8:15–16)

> And because you are sons, God has sent forth the Spirit of His Son into your hearts, crying out, "Abba, Father!" (Gal. 4:6)

In 1996, Bob Carlisle recorded "Butterfly Kisses," a ballad that speaks of the love of a father for his daughter. The song quickly became a best seller; topping song charts not only in North America but around the world. It is rare that a song has such strong international appeal.

But this song evidently touched on something deep within the human heart, common to men and women regardless of nationality or religious persuasion.

Its appeal was vividly apparent to me one day while browsing through a local bookstore. I saw a gift-book version of the "Butterfly Kisses" song displayed at the front of the store, another book version of the song in the children's section, and a woman standing in the youth section, with tears in her eyes, reading a third rendition.

In the gift book Bob Carlisle reflects on the song's enormous success and tells stories about how fathers and daughters have responded. He said, "I get a lot of mail from young girls who try to get me to marry their moms. That used to be a real chuckle because it's so cute, but then I realized they don't want a romance for Mom. They want the dad who is in that song, and that just kills me."

The young girls want the dad in the song. They want a dad who loves them, protects them, is kind and tender toward them. They want a dad who is strong, dependable, and unswerving in his commitment to his family. They want a dad who helps them, mentors them, and is their biggest fan. They want this dad so much that they write to a perfect stranger whose only contact with them has been through a song played on the radio about his love for his own daughter, begging him to marry their moms so that they might have the father of their dreams.

What a poignant demonstration of how deep the human need for being fathered really is! And the longing expressed by these little girls is reminiscent of the longing for Father God who resides in the heart of every Christian.

Romans 8:15 tells us that we did not receive a spirit that makes us a slave again to fear, but we received the Spirit of sonship. In Galatians 4:6 Paul explained that "Because you are sons, God sent the Spirit of his Son into our hearts, the Spirit who calls out, 'Abba, Father'" (NIV).

As Christians, we have received the Spirit of adoption. The word *adoption* (Gr. *huiothesia*), also translated "sonship," refers to the process and status of being a son (Gr. *huioi*), or child, of God. For some of us, the concept of adoption carries the idea of being "second best" because couples often adopt children only after they discover they are unable to bear children of their own. But this is not the concept communicated in the Bible.

In the Roman culture of Paul's day, an adopted child, particularly a son, could have greater prestige and privilege than a natural child. This was because a father's rule over his children was, by law, absolute. If a natural son did not have the skill, character, or other attribute that the father desired, the father could diligently search for a boy available for adoption who demonstrated the desirable qualities. If this boy proved himself worthy, the father could initiate the legal process of adoption. At the father's death a favored adopted son would then inherit the father's title, the majority of the estate, and be the primary progenitor of the family name.

Because of the important implications and privileges of being adopted, the Roman process involved several carefully prescribed legal procedures. To begin, the boy's legal and social relationship to his natural family was totally severed. All previous debts and other obligations were paid and eradicated as if they had never existed. Next the boy was placed permanently into his new family, receiving all the rights and privileges that are bestowed upon one naturally born. For the transaction to be legally binding, it required the presence of seven reputable witnesses who could testify to any challenge of the adoption after the father's death.

You have been chosen by the Father. He has adopted you. This means that:

- Your legal and social relationship to your natural "family" root of sin has been severed.
- All of your sin debts and obligations have been paid and eradicated.
- You have been permanently placed into the family of God and now live in the house of the Father.
- You have received all the rights and privileges associated with being a child of God.

THE SPIRIT SHOWS YOU THAT GOD IS YOUR FATHER

Roman law required multiple witnesses for an adoption to be legal. We know that we have been adopted when God's Spirit joins with our spirit in bearing witness that we are children of God. We cry out to God as Father (Rom. 8:16), and the Holy Spirit in us also cries out to the Father (Gal. 4:6; see also Rom. 8:26). Together they make us conscious of the fact that God is our Father and we are his children.

Your adoption is legal and binding because it has been witnessed by the Holy Spirit. The Bible reinforces the teaching with the names used to refer to this witness to your adoption. Scripture calls the Holy Spirit:

- The Spirit of his Son (Gal. 4:6)
- The Spirit of sonship/adoption (Rom. 8:15)
- The Spirit of your Father (Matt. 10:20)
- The Holy Spirit (Luke 11:13)

THE SPIRIT CALLS AND DRIVES YOU TO INTIMACY WITH THE FATHER

The Spirit in your heart cries out, "Abba, Father" (Rom. 8:15; Gal. 4:6). The verb *cry* indicates a spontaneous expression of intensity, full of emotional depth and longing. It is used in its present tense. Literally "your spirit is even now crying out 'Abba!'" The word often is used in the Gospels of those who cry out under the influence of demons. But in this case it speaks of the unrestrainable heart cry of those controlled by the Spirit of God.

The heart represents a person's whole of the inner being: the mind and the will as well as the center of one's emotions. Thus, under the influence of the Spirit, one's whole being—one's whole heart, mind, soul, and strength—cries out with intense longing to connect with the Father. It is a strong, intense, desperate, felt need that calls you and drives us to the Father's heart.

How strongly do you feel the longing in your heart to connect with God the Father? The intensity of this yearning may be the result of many things. If you sense a deep need, the Father can meet it. If your awareness of needing him seems weak, the good news is it can grow as you get to know him better. If you have been injured in your relationship to your dad, God can be the healing and restoring Father your heart really needs.

NOT A SPIRIT OF FEAR

In Romans 8:15, the Holy Spirit is contrasted with a spirit of bondage to fear. Fear keeps us in bondage and prevents us from getting to know God the Father better. I have known many who were so injured in their experience with their father that fear kept them from seeking God.

Paul tells us that we did not receive a spirit that would produce a sense of fear before God. On the contrary, we received a Spirit that gives us confidence that we are God's children and that we can freely relate to him as Father.

Paul expressed a similar thought to Timothy. He reminded Timothy that Christians receive the Spirit of power and of love and of sound thinking and not the spirit of fear (2 Tim. 1:7). Through the Holy Spirit we have the power to decide whether our relationship to God the Father will be ruled by our fears or whether our fears will be overruled by our response to the Spirit's leading.

I want to encourage you. You do not have to make a giant leap that terrifies you. You can, however, turn from fear to trust in the character of Father God. May I ask you to make the following commitments? Consider writing them on a card or in your journal to remind yourself of the journey to overcome fear and move closer to the Father's heart of God.

- I am making a conscious decision that my relationship with my heavenly Father will not be ruled by my fears.
- I am making a conscious commitment to get to know my heavenly Father better.

ABBA, FATHER

For Jesus, "Father" was the primary and most frequent designation for God. When Jesus spoke of God, he not only used the term "our (or your) Father" (Isa. 63:16, Matt. 5:45; 6:9) that was common to Jews, but he also used the intimate family word for "father" in his native Aramaic language: *abba*. Abba is the modern-day equivalent of *daddy, papa,* or *dear father.*

The use of this word is significant. It speaks of personal relationship. It speaks of intimacy, tenderness, dependence, and a complete lack of fear or anxiety. Jesus enjoyed this type of relationship with his Father. He taught his disciples that they could enjoy the same intimacy with Father God. We, too, can approach God as our dear Father, our Daddy, our Papa. And as we have seen, God has imprinted this desire upon our spirits.

George did not have a good relationship with his father. The beatings and humiliation scarred his self-image. The insecurity crippled him and interfered with his interpersonal relationships. Though

George feared that God would treat him the same way that his earthly father had, he took the risk of getting to know him better. Instead of being rejected, belittled, and punished, George found the affirmation and confidence he needed. His heavenly Father healed the wounds his early father had inflicted and brought him to a place of wholeness, confidence, and joy.

Our spirits long for the Father. There is a void, an empty gap within us that cannot be filled by anything else. An intimate relationship with the Father is the "something more" for which we yearn. But unlike the little girls who responded to the "Butterfly Kisses" song, we do not need to search for a father. Through Jesus we already have entered into relationship with the Father of our dreams.

SOMETHING TO DO

Over the next few days, construct a homemade Father's Day card for Abba, Father God. In it express your heart to him, using whatever words you are comfortable with: *Abba, Father, dear Father, Daddy, Papa*. You may want to look over the last several chapters and include any truths you have learned or commitments you have made. You may feel strange doing this, but I encourage you to give it a try. When you have finished the card, set aside a special time to "present" it to your Father. For example, this could be during a personal quiet time at home, at your church facility, or outside in a park. Present the card to your Father in prayer and spend some time talking to him about your relationship. During this time, do not pray in intercession for others. This is your time to talk to your Father honestly and openly about his fatherhood and your relationship to him. Keep the card in a special place. I will ask you to look at it again in our journey together.

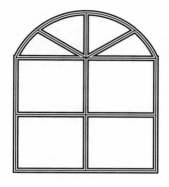

PART 2

Getting to Know God as Father: Father God Is Relationship Oriented

*"Though the mountains be shaken
and the hills be removed,
yet my unfailing love for you will not be shaken
nor my covenant of peace be removed,"
says the LORD, who has compassion on you.*

—ISAIAH 54:10 NIV

"Oh Father, my Father . . . Father God."

Hesitantly, I spoke his name aloud. And then, as if something broke through for me, I found myself trusting that he was indeed hearing me, just as my earthly father had always done.

"Father, oh my Father, God," I cried, with growing confidence. My voice seemed unusually loud in the large bedroom as I knelt on the rug beside my bed. But suddenly that room wasn't empty any more. He was there! I could sense his presence. I could feel his hand laid gently on my head. It was as if I could see his eyes, filled with love and compassion. He was so close that I found myself laying my head on his knees like a little girl sitting at her father's feet. For a long time I knelt there, sobbing quietly, floating in his love. . . .

"I am confused, Father, . . ." I said. "I have to get one thing straight right away." I reached over to the bedside table where I kept the Bible and the Koran side by side. I picked up both books and lifted them, one in each hand. "Which, Father?" I said. "Which one is your book?"

Then a remarkable thing happened. Nothing like it had ever occurred in my life. For I heard a voice inside my being, a voice that spoke to me as clearly as if I were repeating words in my inner mind. They were fresh, full of kindness, yet at the same time full of authority. "In which book do you meet me as your Father?"

—Bilquis Sheikh, Muslim princess

CHAPTER 7

THE FATHER LOVES YOU

My dad was a quiet man. He never talked much. But never has so much love been communicated with so few words. Dad was always there for me, always constant and affirming his love in unspoken ways. If my toys were broken, he would fix them. If I had a cut on my knee, he would bandage it and kiss it better. I remember his big hugs and the feel of his scratchy skin and the smell of his work-smudged red overalls. Dad seemed to have a sixth sense for understanding what was going on in my life. I'll never forget the day I was writing my final accounting exam. About an hour before the exam, I answered the ring of my apartment doorbell to find a vase of rose-buds on the floor in front of the door. The inscription on the card simply said "Dad," but the gesture said so much more. Dad never said, "I love you"— not in so many words. His feelings were so deep that he just couldn't say it. But he would squeeze me tight and with eyes filled with tears would mumble, "You're my girl." And I understood exactly what he was saying.

—Andrea

"Yes, I have loved you with an everlasting love; Therefore with lovingkindness I have drawn you." (Jer. 31:3)

A number of years ago, my husband and I did a short exercise to determine our basic love languages. Love languages are the different ways we express our love for one another. Love can be expressed through words, by serving or doing things for the loved one, by spending time with the loved one, by giving gifts, and/or by physical displays of affection.

The theory behind the exercise is that people express and receive love primarily through their own basic love language. For example, although I express my love for others in all five ways, the primary way I express love is through service. If I really want to show people I love them, I do something for them. Service is also my primary "receptive love language." I appreciate receiving gifts, but to me, when someone serves me, it communicates their love for me in an even more significant way.

My son is different from me. The primary way he expresses his love is through giving. He gives me pieces of gum, a feather, loose change, little trinkets and baubles he finds on his way home, or whatever he has in his pockets. Giving is the primary way he expresses his love, and it is also the expression of love that is the most significant to him. He is overwhelmed if I come home with a little gift for him from the dollar store—not because he craves the gift but because for him the act of giving is the expression of love that means the most.

Understanding the love languages expressed by the various members of my family has helped me to understand and appreciate their expressions of love for me. It has also helped me communicate my love for them in the way that is most meaningful for them. I know beyond a shadow of a doubt that they love me, and they know beyond a shadow of a doubt that I love them.

How does this relate to the love of God? We know God the Father loves us. This is a fact we affirm on an intellectual basis. But do we know and understand and sense the Father's love in our lives on a daily basis? Do we recognize and understand our Father God's language of love?

You can readily apply the principle. Think how certain you are intellectually that God loves you. Then consider to what degree you feel that God loves you. Do you sense a difference between the two? Is there a difference between what you know to be true and what you feel to be true?

King David was one man who really knew the heart of the Father (1 Sam. 13:14; Acts 13:22). His psalms are overflowing with accolades to God's heart of love. "I will sing of the steadfast love of the Lord forever " (Ps. 89:1 ESV). "Your steadfast love is better than life" (Ps. 63:3 ESV).

David was convinced beyond a shadow of a doubt that Father God loved him. It was the thought that was continually on his mind. "Your love is ever before me" (Ps. 26:3 NIV). "By day the LORD directs his love, at night his song is with me" (Ps. 42:8 NIV). "I will be glad and rejoice in your love" (Ps. 31:7 NIV). But how could David be so sure? How could he know with such certainty that he was loved by the Father?

David's secret was that he meditated, studied, and contemplated God's actions. From this he understood the love of God. David said, "The works of the LORD are great, studied by all who have pleasure in them" (Ps. 111:2), and "Whoever is wise, let him heed [pay attention to] these things [God's actions] and consider [understand] the great love of the LORD" (Ps. 107:43 NIV). David was a great lover of God because he studied the great acts of God and thus understood the great love of God.

THE FATHER'S LOVE LANGUAGES

Perhaps your earthly father was awkward in expressing his love for you. Or perhaps he did not communicate his love in a way that you could understand. Your heavenly Father communicates his love for you using all the five love languages mentioned at the beginning of this chapter. He communicates his love through words, through the things he does, through his time and attention, through the gifts he gives and physically, through Jesus—love made flesh. The Father wants you to know, without a doubt, just how much he loves you.

THE FATHER EXPRESSES HIS LOVE FOR YOU IN WORDS

The love of your heavenly Father is the highest and noblest form of love. It is a love that chooses to see something infinitely precious in you. His love also includes concepts of loyalty and faithfulness to his promise. For example, in Deuteronomy 7:6–9, the Father chooses a people to be his special treasure, not because of their attributes but because of his great love. And because he is God, his children can be confident that he will remain faithful to love. He said:

> The Lord your God has chosen you out of all the peoples on
> the face of the earth to be his people, his treasured possession.

The Lord did not choose you and lavish his love on you because you were larger or greater than other nations, for you were the smallest of all nations! It was simply because the Lord loves you, and because he was keeping the oath he had sworn to your ancestors. That is why the Lord rescued you with such amazing power from your slavery under Pharaoh in Egypt. Understand, therefore, that the Lord your God is indeed God. He is the faithful God who keeps his covenant for a thousand generations and constantly loves those who love him and obey his commands. (Deut. 7:7–9 NLT)

Because of the multidimensional nature of God's love, the Hebrew (Old Testament) word used to describe it has been translated in a variety of ways: *love, lovingkindness, mercy, tenderness, unfailing love, kindness,* and/or *grace.* You may find that the verses in your Bible translation use one of these words instead of the specific word *love.*

In the following verses the Father expresses his love for you. As you read them, personalize them by putting your name in the blank.

Jeremiah 31:3: "I have loved _____ with an everlasting love; . . . I have drawn _____ with loving-kindness."

Isaiah 54:10 (NIV): "Though the mountains be shaken and the hills be removed, yet my unfailing love for _____ will not be shaken nor my covenant of peace be removed," says the LORD, who has compassion on _____."

1 John 3:1 (NIV): "How great is the love the Father has lavished on _____, that _____ should be called [a child] of God!"

Do you grasp the significance of this? Do you realize who is speaking? The most high and holy God, Creator of all that is, the Giver of life—immeasurable, immortal, eternal, and all-powerful God—the one who holds oceans in his hands, squeezes the rain from the clouds, scatters stars, splits the skies with lightning, and makes the mountains tremble. This God speaks and says, "Know that I am your Father. You are my treasured, chosen possession. I love you."

Do you truly believe it? If you don't, your lack of belief says much more about what you think about God than what you think about yourself. You may feel insignificant, unattractive, unremarkable, and unworthy, but when your heavenly Father says, "I love you," and you do not believe him, then what you are really saying is "God, you are not big enough to love me," or, "God, you are not good enough to love me," or, "God, you are not being truthful."

The Word of God is powerful. Every word that proceeds from his mouth is accomplished. His word created and sustains the universe. He does not use words lightly. When he speaks, it is so. He cannot lie. Father God says he loves you. Do you believe him? Do you take him at his word?

Growing up, Carlos had never received a hug from his father, nor had he ever heard the words "I love you." By the time Carlos was a man, their relationship was emotionally distant; he and his father rarely spoke. While doing the *In My Father's House* Bible study, Carlos was profoundly impacted by the truth of Father God's love for him. Tears flowed as the Holy Spirit ministered grace and healing into the wounds of his heart. He wrote, "I now know clearly that God the Father loves me. This knowledge has given me a lot of hope, peace, and forgiveness. We have a spectacular Father!" Carlos' newfound awareness of being loved by his heavenly Father transformed his heart. It inspired him to visit his earthly father, embrace him, and say the words, "I love you, Dad." With that simple act, lifelong walls and barriers came crashing down. Accepting the love of his heavenly Father enabled Carlos to begin to build a relationship of love with his earthly dad. What a spectacular father God is!

THE FATHER EXPRESSES HIS LOVE FOR YOU IN THE THINGS HE DOES

> Give thanks to the LORD, for he is good;
> his love endures forever.
> Who can proclaim the mighty acts of the LORD
> or fully declare his praise? (Ps. 106:1–2 NIV)

Andrea was convinced that her dad loved her because of the things he did for her. Have you ever considered that the things God the Father does are actually expressions of his love for you?

King David made a habit of meditating on the acts of God. He saw the love of God in all that God did. According to David, no one could proclaim all of God's acts or fathom the extent of the Father's love. But the wise will "observe these things" to "understand" his love (Ps. 107:43).

The following verses are just a small sample of the types of things the Father does that proclaim his love for you. As you read them, notice the things he does:

He makes grass grow for the cattle,
and plants for man to cultivate—
bringing forth food from the earth:
wine that gladdens the heart of man,
oil to make his face shine,
and bread that sustains his heart.
(Ps. 104:14–15 NIV)

He loads the clouds with moisture;
he scatters his lightning through them.
At his direction they swirl around
over the face of the whole earth
to do whatever he commands them.
He brings the clouds to punish men,
or to water his earth and show his love.
(Job 37:11–13 NIV)

Praise the LORD, O my soul,
and forget not all his benefits—
who forgives all your sins
and heals all your diseases,
who redeems your life from the pit
and crowns you with love and compassion,
who satisfies your desires with good things
so that your youth is renewed like the eagle's.
The LORD works righteousness
and justice for all the oppressed.
(Ps. 103:2–6 NIV)

He predestined us to be adopted as his sons through Jesus
Christ, in accordance with his pleasure and will. (Eph. 1:5 NIV)

But because of his great love for us, God, who is rich in mercy,
made us alive with Christ. (Eph. 2:4–5 NIV)

King David saw a connection between the mighty acts of God and
the love of God. God does many, many things—all of which are an
expression of his love. The Jewish people recognized this. Psalm 136
is known as the "Great Hallel," the great psalm of praise. It was the
portion of Scripture that was recited at family gatherings and special
events. It follows a characteristic pattern. The leader mentions an act
of God, and the rest of the people respond with the conclusion, "His
love endures forever" (NIV). Here are some excerpts:

- He made the great lights. His love endures forever!
- He laid out the earth above the waters. His love endures
  forever!
- He set the sun to rule the day. His love endures forever!
- He led His people through the wilderness. His love endures
  forever!
- He slew Og, King of Bashan. His love endures forever!

In the Great Hallel, God's people conclude that the acts of God are
an indicator of the Father's love. Do you make this same connection in
your mind? When you see a crimson sunset, tiny rainbows bursting
from the dew droplets on a leaf, when a great eagle flaps its wings
overhead or a startled hedgehog waddles across your path, do you
make the connection? When the rain comes and waters your garden
and the tiny seeds break open and tender green shoots poke their
heads through the surface of the dirt, when you savor the sweetness of
a ripe strawberry, do you make the right connection? Do you conclude, "His love endures forever!" God's acts are an indicator of his
love for you. Are you getting the message?

Can you think of any other things the Father has specifically done
for you that demonstrate his love for you? I consider numerous things
every day as specific gifts from my Father. The mountains of my
homeland in Canada glisten with the Father's gifts—sometimes white
with snow, sometimes robed in the many colors of summer. Every day
echoes the words of Jeremiah, "Because of the LORD's great love we are

not consumed, for his compassions never fail. They are new every morning; great is your faithfulness" (Lam. 3:22–23).

THE FATHER EXPRESSES HIS LOVE FOR YOU IN TIME AND ATTENTION

As I have talked to people about their relationships with their earthly dads, almost all of them commented on the absence or presence of their dad's time and attention. "My dad was always there for me," or "My dad was always so busy; he rarely paid any attention to me." Most people regard the attentiveness of their fathers as an indicator of how much their fathers love them.

Your heavenly Father demonstrates that he loves you deeply by devoting his time and attention to you. Consider some of the things Scripture says about our heavenly Father's attention:

The Father is always there to help you: "God is our refuge and strength, an ever-present help in trouble" (Ps. 46:1 NIV).

Remember a time of seeing a father help a toddler learning to walk? David applied the image to the heavenly Father: "You hold me by my right hand" (Ps. 73:23).

What greater image of personalized attention can you find than these words from Jesus? "Even the very hairs of your head are all numbered" (Matt. 10:30 NIV).

The Father responds when you call to him: "The righteous cry out, and the LORD hears them; he delivers them from all their troubles" (Ps. 34:17 NIV).

Are you hungry for someone to value you enough to give you their time and attention? Then consider this truth:

He will not let your foot slip—
he who watches over you will not slumber;
indeed, he who watches over Israel
will neither slumber nor sleep.
The LORD watches over you—
the LORD is your shade at your right hand;
the sun will not harm you by day,
nor the moon by night.
The LORD will keep you from all harm—
he will watch over your life;

the LORD will watch over your coming and going
both now and forevermore. (Ps. 121:3–8 NIV)

He is there, and he is involved. Your heavenly Father has never
missed a piano recital, soccer game, school play, or awards ceremony.
He has never been too busy or distracted to be there or to pay attention to you. When you talk, he listens. When you cry, he comforts.
When you ask, he answers. When you leave the path, he directs you
back. When you draw near, he draws near. When you extend your
hand, he holds it. When you listen, he speaks. He is always there,
interested and involved in your life. Father God will never leave and
never forsake you. That's his promise (Ps. 73:23).

THE FATHER EXPRESSES HIS LOVE FOR YOU IN THE GIFTS HE GIVES

Fathers love to give gifts to their children. I always am amazed at
the absolute delight my husband feels in picking out gifts for our sons.
He takes an incredible amount of time in the aisles of the toy or sports
store, clicking, whirring, zooming, squeezing, and bouncing his selec-
tions until he finds just the right one.

My father was a carpenter. He often gave me gifts that he had built
in his workshop. One such gift was a pretty white doll cradle with
spindles along the sides and cutout heart-shaped handles on either
end. It remains in the attic to this day. Did your earthly father ever give
you a special gift? If so, what was it?

Jesus pointed out that even fathers who are sinful have the ability
to give good gifts to their children. How much more, he reasoned, does
our perfect, heavenly Father give his children good gifts? (Matt. 7:11).
David said, "The LORD will indeed give what is good" (Ps. 85:12 NIV).
The Father gives you gifts to demonstrate his love for you.

The following passages describe some of the good gifts he gives.

He has made everything beautiful in its time. He has also set
eternity in the hearts of men; yet they cannot fathom what
God has done from beginning to end. I know that there is
nothing better for men than to be happy and do good while
they live. That everyone may eat and drink, and find satisfaction in all his toil—this is the gift of God. (Eccl. 3:11–13 NIV)

Did you note the gifts of beauty, having eternity in our hearts, happiness, the ability to do good, and to find satisfaction in work?

> Moreover, when God gives any man wealth and possessions, and enables him to enjoy them, to accept his lot and be happy in his work—this is a gift of God. He seldom reflects on the days of his life, because God keeps him occupied with gladness of heart. (Eccl. 5:19–20)

Were you surprised to see that God intends for people to enjoy possessions? What difference does it make in your view of your heavenly Father to know he wants you to be happy and experience gladness of heart?

Ephesians 2:8 tells us that salvation is a gift from God, and 1 Corinthians 12:11 informs us that spiritual gifts come from him. God so thoroughly shows his love through gifts that James wrote: "Every good and perfect gift is from above, coming down from the Father of the heavenly lights, who does not change like shifting shadows" (James 1:17 NIV). God is not stingy, nor does he delight in withholding from his children. No, on the contrary, our heavenly Father delights to give his children gifts.

THE FATHER EXPRESSES HIS LOVE FOR YOU THROUGH JESUS, GOD MADE FLESH

> The kindness and love of God our Savior appeared.
> (Titus 3:4 NIV)

Titus 3:4 teaches that the kindness and love of God appeared physically, in the flesh, through his Son, Jesus. Physical affection is the final language of love. Although the Father is not physically present to give us hugs, his ultimate expression of love for us is a physical one. Jesus, who came from the Father, "became flesh and dwelt among us" (John 1:14 ESV). Jesus is the physical expression of the Father's love, the Father's ultimate expression of love.

One of the most amazing things to me about Jesus is how much he loved to touch people and how much they loved to touch him. Jesus touched the young and the old, babies, friends, disciples, men, and women. He even touched the untouchable in love.

Remember the story about the man with leprosy who came to Jesus? Throwing himself down at Jesus' feet, the man cried out, "Lord, If You are willing, You can make me clean" (Matt. 8:2). The rest of the crowd had scattered. They were afraid to be close to a leper. Not a person was willing to touch him. But Scripture records that, filled with compassion, Jesus reached out his hand and touched the man. "I am willing," Jesus said (Matt. 8:3).

I think of the crowds who were always pressing close to Jesus, the children who wanted to clamber on his lap and the hemorrhaging woman who at great risk reached out to touch his garment. Hebrews 1:3 says that Jesus is the radiance of God's glory and the exact representation of his being. Jesus loved to touch people, and he never refused to touch those who reached out to touch him. If this is the case, does it not follow that the Father himself would love to give and receive hugs?

When Jesus was on earth, he demonstrated the Father's love physically, through touch. But the ultimate expression of love was when Jesus physically died on the cross to reconcile us to the Father: "This is how God showed his love among us: He sent his one and only Son into the world that we might live through him. This is love: not that we loved God, but that he loved us and sent his Son as an atoning sacrifice for our sins" (1 John 4:9–10). Jesus displayed the love of the Father in a physical, visible way, so that we, too, might know and believe the Father's love for us (John 15:9; 17:23, 26).

YOU CAN KNOW WITH CERTAINTY THAT THE FATHER LOVES YOU

According to David, those who are wise will pay attention to God's love languages and grow to understand the great love of the Lord. He said, "Within your temple, O God, we meditate on your unfailing love" (Ps. 48:9 NIV). Meditation is close or continued thought, the revolving of a subject in the mind. David exercised the discipline of meditating on the love of God and therefore became a great lover of God. David loved the Father because he knew how much the Father loved him (1 John 4:19).

You, too, can grow in your understanding of how much the Father loves you by meditating on how he has communicated his love through his love languages. By meditating on his love, you can know with certainty that God the Father loves you.

May I suggest an action you can take to close this chapter? Take a few minutes to compose and pray your own personal Hallel. Look over what you have read and identify specific ways the Father demonstrates his love for you and then respond with the conclusion, "Your love for me endures forever."

I hope that this chapter reinforced for you the fact that you can know how much the Father loves you by studying and contemplating his actions. He expresses his love for you in words, in the things he does, in the time and attention he gives, in the gifts he gives, and in Jesus, his love made flesh.

The Father's love for you endures forever.

CHAPTER 8

THE FATHER CROWNS YOU WITH HIS LOVE

If you care for me
speak to me without words
in a spiral of starlings
thrown into a bank of wind, scarves
of an invisible dancer making the sky a stage

Make a negligent gesture like
the drop of a chestnut at my feet
the glossy nucula bounding out of its spiky casing
rolling to me, a gift round
and brown as a chocolate cream

Caress me with a curtain of dew
on my moonlit skylight, or boulders
shining under their clear skin
of rain. In the rock garden
a crimson cosmos articulates
its bright, small world. Speak
to my eyes in syllables of light
and color, if you care for me

Remind me about space as
I watch the finches
peck at the wind in the balsams. The doe
cleaves the air current over
the ribbon of creek. The great
blue heron elbows its way up
through gaps wild with branches
and you are opening
for me, too, a new passage
between the trees

By the way you breathe dead leaves
into a small whirlwind of fire
show me, if you care for me, how you can
lift me from the dust,
light me like tinder

—Lucy Shaw[1]

And we have known and believed the love that God has for us.
God is love, and he who abides in love abides in God, and God
in him. . . . We love Him because He first loved us.
(1 John 4:16, 19)

I will declare that your love stands firm forever, that you established your faithfulness in heaven itself. (Ps. 89:2 NIV)

Luci Shaw's poem at the beginning of the chapter demonstrates
how we can observe God's love for us in the very things that we regard
as ordinary or insignificant. We can be wise and see the love of God in
these things, or we can totally miss the message.

This is the second chapter in which we will reflect upon the
Father's heart of love for his daughters and sons. Our goal is that we,
like David and the early believers, may "know" and "believe" the love
that the Father has for us (1 John 4:16).

Why do you suppose it is often so difficult for people to accept
the fact that God the Father loves them? And how about you? Do you
find it difficult to accept the fact that God the Father loves you? In
2 Thessalonians 3:5 the apostle Paul prays, "May the Lord direct your
hearts into the love of God." To *direct* means "to guide straight
toward." Take a moment to pray this for yourself. Pray that the Lord

will direct your heart into the love of God so that you may know and believe the love that the Father has for you.

CHARACTERISTICS OF THE FATHER'S LOVE

In the previous chapter we learned that God the Father loves us and that he communicates his love in various ways. Now we will examine the specific characteristics of the Father's love. The Bible teaches us that his love is great, dependable, eternal, and bigger than we can ever think or imagine.

The Father's Love Is Great

The definition of the word *great* is "unusually or comparatively large in size or dimensions; considerable in degree; beyond what is ordinary; notable or remarkable; of noble or superior character." The Bible uses the word *great* to describe the Father's love. His love is so great, so marvelous, that the writers of the Bible struggled to find words to describe it. In Ephesians 3:14–21, Paul says that the love of the Father defies knowledge. It is too great to appreciate or understand fully. If Paul were writing today, he might have used the expression: "It blows my mind!"

Paul said that the love of the Father was incomprehensible to the human mind. But to Paul this was not an excuse to give up trying to understand it. On the contrary, this was reason to pursue it all the more. Paul prayed that believers might be able to grasp the dimensions—the width and length and depth and height—of God's love so that they might be filled with all the fullness of the Father.

According to Paul, expanding our understanding of the love of God enlarges our capacity to know and relate to God and to be filled with him. This was David's secret. David meditated on the love of God so much that he became "a man after [God's] own heart" (1 Sam. 13:14; Acts 13:22).

Look at some of the ways the writers of Scripture described the love of God. The Father's love is:

Ephesians 2:4	A great love
Ephesians 3:19	A love that surpasses knowledge
Psalm 69:16	A love that is full of goodness
Hosea 11:4	A love that binds us with kindness

Psalm 31:21	A wonderful love
Psalm 36:7	A priceless love
Psalm 36:7	An unfailing love
Psalm 63:3	A love that is better than life itself

That list of descriptions of God's love blows my mind. It simply amazes me that the Creator of the universe is filled with such love and that he longs for me to know and experience how great—how exceedingly extraordinary and remarkable—his love for me really is.

The Father's Love Is Dependable

Of all the descriptions of the love of the Father, the most common is that his love is "unfailing" (Ps. 6:4; 13:5; 33:5; 36:7; 48:9; 90:14; 107:15; 130:7; 147:11 NIV). This means that the Father's love is consistent and dependable. Psalm 89:2 (NIV) says that his love "stands firm."

Earthly fathers are not perfect in their love. They have bad days. They can disappoint us through inconsistency, through undependability, or because of circumstances beyond their control. Their love can fail.

Think of all the things that can separate you from the love of your earthly father. You could include everything from obsession with work to divorce, from depression to death. Then compare those things to the words of Romans 8:38–39.

> For I am convinced that neither death nor life, neither angels nor demons, neither the present nor the future, nor any powers, neither height nor depth, nor anything else in all creation, will be able to separate us from the love of God that is in Christ Jesus our Lord. (Rom. 8:38–39 NIV)

Your heavenly Father will never fail you. He is totally dependable in every circumstance and at every time. His love will not fail you. Not ever.

Have you ever felt let down or disappointed by God the Father? According to Scripture (Rom. 8:38–39), the love of the Father will never fail us. In light of this, can you think of another reason for your disappointment? A friend told me how angry she had been because she believed God let her down. Later she realized the Father simply did not do what she wanted him to, when she wanted him to do it. She said at the time she could see no good in her situation. But later events showed her how fortunate she had been that God did not surrender to her selfish demands.

David knew the agony and questions of pain. "How long, O Lord? Will you forget me forever? How long will you hide your face from me? How long must I wrestle with my thoughts and every day have sorrow in my heart?" (Ps. 13:1–2 NIV).

But David had studied the love of God, and his confidence in the love of the Father was unshakable. Despite his questions, in his next breath he acknowledged the dependability of God's love. "I trust in your unfailing love; my heart rejoices in your salvation. I will sing to the LORD, for he has been good to me" (Ps. 13:5–6 NIV).

Like David, you can be assured of the dependability of the Father's love, even in the midst of your pain and suffering. His love will not fail you. Not ever.

The Father's Love Is Eternal

How long is forever? David likened forever to "as long as the sun, as long as the moon" (Ps. 72:5 NIV). One of my sons likened it to "until the Great Sahara Desert is covered with rain forest." Another likened it to "until our dog stops chewing up our backyard." What does forever call to mind for you? Whatever image comes to mind, the description undoubtedly falls short.

The Father's love will outlast all the images we can muster. David tells us that the love of God endures forever (Ps. 100:5). It is from everlasting to everlasting (Ps. 103:17). God himself assures us of the eternal nature of his love (Jer. 31:3). His love for you began before the creation of the world (Eph. 1:4–5) and will continue for the rest of your life. It will continue through all the generations of your offspring; it will continue until the end of time and beyond. The Father's love for you will never end.

THE UNFATHOMABLE MAGNITUDE OF THE FATHER'S LOVE

In the 1970s and 1980s, shoppers could buy cute porcelain statues that had their arms spread out as wide as possible. On the chests of the statues were red, plastic, heart-shaped plaques that declared

"I love you this much!" The idea was that the giver loved the person receiving the statue to the full extent, as much as they possibly could. Given the arm span of the average person, the maximum amount of human love possible measured in at a distance of about six feet.

Let's compare that human measure of love capacity to the capacity of the love of the Father. How much does Father God love you? Paul prayed that we would be able to grasp the dimensions, how wide and long and high and deep his love is (Eph. 3:18–19). David gives us some practical suggestions for measuring it. He said that the earth is filled with the love of God and that God's love is as high as the heavens are above the earth (Ps. 119:64; 36:5; 103:11).

If we go by the first suggestion of God's love "filling the earth," it would cover an area of approximately 196,951,000 square miles. If we take into consideration the mass of the earth, his love would weigh approximately 6.6 sextillion tons (6,600,000,000,000,000,000,000,000).

And what of the second suggestion? Just how high are the heavens above the Earth? If David meant the moon, the distance from the Earth to the moon is approximately 250,000 miles. That is about the same distance as ten trips around the equator, or 220 million adult men standing with arms outstretched, fingertip to fingertip. The distance to the sun is roughly four hundred times further.

The nearest star in our galaxy, Alpha Centauri, is 4.3 light years away. A light year is 5.88 trillion miles. So if you could travel the distance from the Earth to the moon every day, it would take almost three hundred years to reach the nearest star. That would be nearly a quadrillion adult men standing fingertip to fingertip.

The nearest galaxy, the Great Andromeda Galaxy, known as the sister galaxy to the Milky Way and part of our "local group" of galaxies, is two million light years away from the edge of our galaxy. If we could leave from the edge of our galaxy, it would take 437,500 years of traveling the distance from the Earth to the moon every day to reach the Great Andromeda. That is more adult men standing fingertip to fingertip than I have the numeric vocabulary to express. And astronomers hypothesize that there are thousands upon thousands of such galaxies in the universe.

The height of the heavens above the Earth is so staggering as to be incomprehensible.

Of course, the Father's love, like human love, cannot really be measured. David's suggestions are figurative, not literal. But quantifying the love of the Father in comparison with our human capacity to love does point to an important truth. God's love for you is untold times bigger than the best, most devoted love of any human. The magnitude of his love is so large as to be incomprehensible.

In describing how much he loves you, your Father, the Creator, stretches out his arms to the right and the left, past all the galaxies of the universe, and says to you, "I love you this much."

LAVISHED WITH LOVE

The apostle John exclaims, "How great is the love the Father has lavished on us" (1 John 3:1 NIV). To *lavish* means "to give freely and profusely." The word indicates an exceedingly liberal, abundant, and extravagant outpouring. David says that the Lord is "rich" in love (Ps. 145:8 NIV). Paul notes that from his riches, the Father "poured" out his love into our hearts (Rom. 5:5).

Imagine the following exercise to demonstrate visibly how the Father lavishes his love on you: Put an empty cup into your kitchen sink. Now fill the largest pitcher you have with water. Slowly begin to pour the water into the empty cup. Continue pouring until the pitcher is empty. As you do this, imagine that you are the empty cup and that the water is the love of the Father.

RESULTS OF UNDERSTANDING THE FATHER'S LOVE

The Father "crowns" you with his love (Ps. 103:4). A crown is a mark of victory or distinction. It signifies power and dominion.

When you were little, did you ever dream of being royalty and wearing a crown? Not only are you royalty through Jesus (1 Pet. 2:9), but the Father's love can crown you with victory over turmoil, insecurity, insignificance, depression, hopelessness, worry, doubt, or fear. His crown is a mark of distinction which, when recognized, has the ability to produce the following characteristics in your life:

Zephaniah 3:17	Quiet peace
Psalm 21:7	Trust
Psalm 21:7	Unshakability

Psalm 94:18	Steadfastness
Psalm 31:7	Gladness and joy
Psalm 33:18	Hope
Psalm 59:16	Strength
Psalm 119:76	Comfort
Psalm 122:6	Security
Psalm 138:8	Confidence
1 John 4:16	Absence of fear

Which of the above characteristics would you like to see more of in your life? I believe that understanding the Father's love for you can increase these characteristics in you. The more you rejoice in the Father's unfailing love, the more you will find stability growing in your life as well. That stability may surprise you by showing up when life seems to shake.

KEEP YOURSELF IN THE LOVE OF THE FATHER

The early believers "knew" and "believed" the love that the Father had for them (1 John 4:16). Jude encouraged them to "keep" themselves in the love of God (Jude 21). To "keep" means "to watch over, take care of, keep an eye on, observe intently." After studying the love of the Father in the past two chapters, you "know" how much he loves you. But in order to "believe" it, you must take care to "keep" yourself in his love.

May I ask you to end this chapter in prayer? Ask the Father to direct your heart into his love. Make a commitment to keep yourself in the love of God.

CHAPTER 9

THE FATHER IS KIND AND GENTLE

My father was a harsh man, a strict disciplinarian, unable to show love or affection. I do not recall happy days as a child. We learned responsibility, commitment, honesty, and self-discipline; but we did not learn acceptance, appreciation, kindness, and forgiveness. Over the years I've had to struggle with the idea that God the Father is kind, for I did not experience kindness from my own father.

—Kathy

I will tell of the kindnesses of the LORD,
the deeds for which he is to be praised,
according to all the LORD has done for us—
yes, the many good things he has done . . .
according to his compassion and many kindnesses.
(Isa. 63:7 NIV)

One of the reasons people, and especially women, struggle to accept the Father's love is that they do not truly believe that the Father is kind. To be kind is "to be of a good or benevolent nature or disposition." It means that a person's basic nature toward others is pleasant and agreeable. Gentleness is an extension of kindness. It means to be kind in manner as well as disposition, in actions as well as attitude.

Let me ask you a couple of questions, and I want you to think about what you feel rather than what you think. Do you feel that God the Father is basically kind and benevolent? Or do you feel that he is basically harsh and punitive?

I have dealt with many believers who testify to a major disconnect between what they know to be true and what they feel. They know and believe facts about God, but their hearts tell them something entirely different.

The issue represents one of life's key issues. Is God kind and benevolent or harsh and punitive? Part of the difficulty comes from the fact that God sometimes acts in a clearly loving way, while at other times God can appear extremely harsh. A kind person can also, if necessary, dispense discipline.

If, like me, you are a parent, you probably know this from personal experience. At heart I am a kind mother. I love my children deeply. But that does not mean I do not judge my children's wrong behavior and punish them for it. Although I am kind, my love for my children demands that I discipline them. But the discipline I administer is only momentary, and it is never unfounded or unpredictable. It is balanced and directed by my love and my basic disposition of kindness toward them.

In order to understand God the Father, we must understand that he loves us and that his basic disposition toward us is one of kindness. He delights in kindness. But, in a way similar to how I function as a parent, the Father's kindness does not rule out the possibility of discipline. The Father delights in kindness, but he also delights in justice and righteousness. "'But let him who boasts boast about this: that he understands and knows me, that I am the LORD, who exercises kindness, justice and righteousness on the earth, for in these I delight,' declares the Lord" (Jer. 9:24 NIV).

Job's friends and even Job himself misunderstood the character of the Father. When he experienced trials, he wrongly concluded that God was out to get him. He thought God was a punitive judge, just waiting for someone to do wrong so that he could unleash the fury and full power of punishment on the wrongdoer.

Job even insinuated that the Father took some perverse pleasure in oppressing those who were righteous (Job 10:3, 13–17). In the end Job discovered that he was wrong and repented of his attitude. He had totally misunderstood the character of God (Job 42:4–6).

Jonah, in contrast to Job, was fully aware of the kindness of God. But Jonah hated the people of Nineveh and wanted God to punish them for their wickedness. The reason he ran away—and was swallowed by the fish—was not because he was afraid of the people; it was because he resented the kindness of God. Jonah knew that if the Ninevites showed even the least bit of response to God's message, God would quickly turn and be kind to them.

"I knew that you are a gracious and compassionate God, slow to anger and abounding in love, a God who relents from sending calamity. . . . That is why I was so quick to flee to Tarshish" (Jon. 4:2 NIV). Jonah resented the Father's kindness. He knew that kindness was the Father's basic disposition. "Yet the LORD longs to be gracious to you; he rises to show you compassion" (Isa. 30:18 NIV).

God the Father is kind. He delights in kindness and continually exercises kindness. He even shows kindness to those who are undeserving and/or ungrateful (Luke 6:35; Acts 14:17). Kindness is a hallmark of his character.

The kindness of my heavenly Father reminds me of an experience I had with my earthly father. My dad did not hesitate to discipline me when I was willfully disobedient or rebellious, but he was always kind.

When I was sixteen, just after I got my driver's license, I took the family station wagon to the store to pick up some things. When I came out of the store, two cars were parked extremely close to the wagon. I was, essentially, sandwiched in. I was not skilled enough to maneuver out of the parking space and ended up putting a huge dent in the door and a massive scratch down the whole side of the wagon. Thankfully, the other cars were not damaged at all.

I distinctly remember showing my father the damage. I was in tears, and between sobs I managed to say, "Dad, look what I did to your car! It's all bent in!" I felt that I deserved punishment for what I had done.

But Dad in his kindness just looked at me, smiled, put his arm around my shoulder, and said, "Well then, I guess I'll just have to bend it out again." Which he did. He did not belittle, mock, or shame me for my incompetence, nor did he allow me to pay for the repairs. His behavior was full of kindness, for he is a kind man.

Father God is a kind God. He has promised that though the mountains depart and the hills be removed, his kindness shall not depart from you. If he is angered, it lasts but a moment. If you bent it in, he is willing and eager to bend it out again. His kindness lasts forever.

You see God's disposition of love for you everywhere in Scripture. For example, look at these words from Isaiah:

"For a brief moment I abandoned you,
but with deep compassion I will bring you back.
In a surge of anger
I hid my face from you for a moment,
but with everlasting kindness
I will have compassion on you," says the LORD your
    Redeemer.
"To me this is like the days of Noah,
when I swore that the waters of Noah would never again
    cover the earth.
So now I have sworn not to be angry with you,
never to rebuke you again.
Though the mountains be shaken
and the hills be removed,
yet my unfailing love for you will not be shaken
nor my covenant of peace be removed,"
says the LORD, who has compassion on you.
(Isa. 54:7–10 NIV)

The Father's disposition toward you is one of kindness. "You are forgiving and good, O Lord, abounding in love to all who call to you" (Ps. 86:5 NIV).

THE FATHER'S WAY OF GENTLENESS

The Father is not only kind in disposition but also gentle in manner. Gentleness is his usual way. First Kings 19 tells us of one of Elijah the prophet's critical encounters with God:

The LORD said, "Go out and stand on the mountain in the presence of the LORD, for the LORD is about to pass by."

Then a great and powerful wind tore the mountains apart and shattered the rocks before the LORD, but the LORD was not in the wind. After the wind there was an earthquake, but the LORD was not in the earthquake. After the earthquake came a fire, but the LORD was not in the fire. And after the fire came a gentle whisper. (vv. 11–12 NIV)

In this passage Elijah experienced the Father's presence, but the Father revealed himself in a way we would never have guessed. Rather than in the dramatic power of wind or fire, God chose to reveal himself to Elijah in a still, small voice instead. Gentleness is the Father's way.

The Father told Jesus what to do during Christ's time on Earth. Jesus said, "I do exactly what my Father has commanded me" (John 14:31 NIV). According to Isaiah 42:3 (NIV), the Father's directives were that "a bruised reed he will not break, and a smoldering wick he will not snuff out." What an indication of the gentleness of the Father! As Paul wrote in Romans 2:4, it is the kindness of God that leads us toward repentance.

Gentle with His Children

A beautiful passage that demonstrates the Father's heart of kindness toward his children appears in the writings of the prophet Hosea:

> When Israel was a child, I loved him,
> And out of Egypt I called My son. . . .
> I taught Ephraim to walk,
> Taking them by their arms;
> But they did not know that I healed them.
> I drew them with gentle cords,
> With bands of love,
> And I was to them as those who take the yoke from
>   their neck.
> I stooped and fed them. (Hos. 11:1, 3–4)

What an astounding picture of the Father's heart! The Father is not harsh or cruel to his child. On the contrary, he gently takes you by your arms, teaching you to walk. He heals you, draws you close, relieves your burdens, stoops and feeds you. He does this, even when you are unaware of the tender love and kindness he has toward you.

CHAPTER 10

THE FATHER IS WITH YOU

I remember standing in front of the huge oak door of my father's office. Papa often worked at home. And when he was working, the massive door, which normally stood wide open, was almost closed. I say "almost" because Papa always left it slightly ajar. I would stand at the crack, peeking in, not wanting to disturb him for fear that Mama would scold me. Somehow, Papa knew when I was there. Without even looking up, he would say, "Hello, Princess!" Then he would put down his glasses and motion for me to come to him. I would squeeze through the crack, push the heavy door closed, and run to his open arms. The stiff leather on the chair creaked as I jumped into his lap. Papa would ask, "And how is the world treating you today?" He always listened carefully, giving me his full attention. No detail seemed too small or too insignificant. Papa was interested in every detail of my life.

When I grew to be a woman, I heard about the God who was a loving Father. I was immediately drawn to him. Just imagine. The God of the universe wanted to relate to me like my papa. The thought was overwhelming.

—Arianna

Where can I flee from Your presence?
If I ascend into heaven, You are there;
If I make my bed in hell, behold, You are there.
If I take the wings of the morning,
And dwell in the uttermost parts of the sea,
Even there Your hand shall lead me,
And Your right hand shall hold me. (Ps. 139:7–10)

As for me, You uphold me in my integrity,
And set me before Your face forever. (Ps. 41:12)

Draw near to God and He will draw near to you.
(James 4:8)

Heather, a friend of mine who is a single mom, came over for coffee a few days ago. Her two-year-old daughter, Emma, was playing gleefully on the kitchen floor. I commented on how much fun it was for me to watch Emma learn new things and to listen to her begin to chatter. A shadow passed over Heather's face. She blinked back tears and said, "I wish her father thought so. He hasn't seen her in over a year and doesn't even ask about her."

How sad. Instinctively, we know that there is something not right about a father who is not present and does not want to be involved in the life of his own daughter. A father should be there. A father should care.

In your life, do you feel that God the Father is present and near, or do feel that he is aloof and distant? Your feelings may be a result of your experience with your earthly father rather than the reality of your heavenly Father. The most astounding thing about our faith is that God promised to be with us. "I will dwell among you, and I will be your God," is the covenant of love he made with the nation of Israel. (see Exod. 6:7; 29:45–46). "My Presence will go with you, and I will give you rest" (Exod. 33:14).

Moses taught that the abiding presence of God was the mark that distinguished God's people from all the other people on the face of the earth (Exod. 33:14–15). He asked, "What other nation has their gods near them the way the LORD our God is near us?" (Deut. 4:7 NIV).

The presence of God was evident in the pillar of cloud and the pillar of fire. According to Exodus 13:22, "Neither the pillar of cloud by day nor the pillar of fire by night left its place in front of the people" (NIV). The Father's presence was always there.

God then instructed Moses to construct the tabernacle as a portable dwelling place for the presence of God (Exod. 25:8). The tabernacle was also called "the tent of meeting," for it was the place where God met man. The presence of God above the tabernacle was visible to the people of Israel "throughout all their journeys" (Exod. 40:38 NIV).

Later, when King Solomon constructed a permanent temple, the cloud of God's presence came and filled it (1 Kings 8:10). Solomon had built the magnificent temple as a place for God to dwell "forever" (1 Kings 8:13). But even he wondered, "Will God indeed dwell on the earth? Behold, heaven and the heaven of heavens cannot contain You. How much less this temple which I have built!" (1 Kings 8:27).

In Old Testament times the Father's presence was with his people in a visible or symbolic way, through smoke, clouds, or objects like the ark of the covenant. But the book of Hebrews teaches us that the tabernacle, the temple, and all the artifacts and customs were only shadows of the good things that were to come (Heb. 9–10). They pointed to the time when the Father's promise of his presence would be fulfilled in an even better way.

"I will live with them and walk among them, and I will be their God, and they will be my people. . . . I will be a Father to you, and you will be my sons and daughters" (2 Cor. 6:16, 18 NIV).

The Father's promise was fulfilled through his Son Jesus, also called Immanuel, which means, "God with us" (Hag. 2:6–9). It was further fulfilled through the Father's gift of the Holy Spirit (Joel 2:28), the Spirit of his Son in our hearts who calls out, "Abba, Father" (Gal. 4:6).

Look with me at some of the clear teachings of Scripture concerning the presence of God:

- God lives in temples, but not the kind built by hands. (Acts 17:24)
- "We are the temple of the living God." (2 Cor. 6:16 NIV)

The following members of the Trinity live in each believer:

- The Spirit of God lives in you. (John 14:17)
- Jesus lives in you. (John 14:20)
- Along with Jesus, God the Father makes his home in you. (John 14:23)

God the Father is not an absent father. He does not go to the office and forget about you. He does not go away on long trips. He does not walk out and leave. The Father is always with you.

If what we've seen isn't enough, look at what these Scriptures clearly state:

Yet I am always with you; you hold me by my right hand. (Ps. 73:23 NIV)

The Lord is near to all who call on him, to all who call on him in truth. (Ps. 145:18 NIV).

In my integrity you uphold me and set me in your presence forever. (Ps. 41:12 NIV)

The Father makes a promise to be with you always (Deut. 31:7; Heb. 13:5 NIV). Personalize the promise by reading your own name in the following blanks.

"Be strong and courageous. I will go with _____; never will I leave _____; never will I forsake _____."

WELCOMING THE NEARNESS OF THE FATHER

The Father is with his children. He likes being with his children. This is an astounding truth. The reality of his presence with us, like his love for us, is a concept that is so big that we can hardly grasp it. In Psalm 139:1–6, David reflects on the reality of God's presence: "Such knowledge is too wonderful for me; It is high, I cannot attain it!" (v. 6).

Close your eyes and imagine that God the Father is right beside you. How do you feel about the idea of the Father's nearness? Do you feel happy? Frightened? Indifferent? Unworthy? Intimidated? Secure? Peaceful? Do you welcome his nearness, or do you feel uncomfortable with the thought?

How you feel about the nearness of the Father is undoubtedly influenced by your experience with your earthly father. It also is influenced by your understanding of the holiness of God, of redemption and of grace. But regardless of how you feel, the Bible teaches that the Father is with his children. He is "not far," even from those who aren't his (Acts 17:27).

According to Paul, the Father wants people to seek him and reach out for him (Acts 17:27). He desires to be close to us and to father us. He wants us to welcome his nearness. "How gladly would I treat you like sons. . . . I thought you would call me 'Father' and not turn away from following me" (Jer. 3:19 NIV).

The Father is near. But we must also "draw near" to him in order to sense his presence (James 4:8). To close this chapter, pray through

Psalm 139:1–18. Acknowledge the presence of the Father and tell him that you would like to draw closer to him.

> O LORD, you have searched me / and you know me. You know when I sit and when I rise; / you perceive my thoughts from afar. / You discern my going out and my lying down; / you are familiar with all my ways. / Before a word is on my tongue / you know it completely, O LORD. / You hem me in—behind and before; / you have laid your hand upon me. / Such knowledge is too wonderful for me, / too lofty for me to attain. / Where can I go from your Spirit? / Where can I flee from your presence? / If I go up to the heavens, you are there; / if I make my bed in the depths, you are there; / If I rise on the wings of the dawn, / if I settle on the far side of the sea, / even there your hand will guide me, / your right hand will hold me fast. / If I say, "Surely the darkness will hide me / and the light become night around me," / even the darkness will not be dark to you; / the night will shine like the day, / for darkness is as light to you. / For you created my inmost being; / you knit me together in my mother's womb. / I praise you because I am fearfully and wonderfully made; / your works are wonderful, / I know that full well. / My frame was not hidden from you / when I was made in the secret place. / When I was woven together in the depths of the earth, / your eyes saw my unformed body. / All the days ordained for me / were written in your book / before one of them came to be. / How precious to me are your thoughts, O God! / How vast is the sum of them! / Were I to count them, / they would outnumber the grains of sand. / When I awake, / I am still with you.
> (Ps. 139:1–18 NIV)

CHAPTER 11

THE FATHER IS YOUR FRIEND

My Dad often took me places—to the zoo, swimming, to the park. But he usually invited his friend and his friend's daughter to come along. The two dads would give us money or a treat and scoot us off to play while they sat together and talked. I liked being with Jody, we had good times together, but I felt as though Dad really wasn't all that interested in me. He was there, but he really wasn't "there." Dad was a hard worker, a good provider and protector, and I know that he loves me. But I feel as though I don't really know him. Our relationship seems very superficial. He is my father, but he isn't a close friend.

I think that my relationship with God the Father is the same way. I am certain of his protection, provision, and presence, and I know that he cares about me. But to be truthful, I am not convinced that he is really interested in me. There is a barrier between us. I cannot say that I feel that the Father is my close friend.

—*Lynn*

"See, I have inscribed you on the palms of My hands; Your walls are continually before Me." (Isa. 49:16)

There is a friend who sticks closer than a brother. (Prov. 18:24 NIV)

"Yet the LORD longs to be gracious to you;
he rises to show you compassion." (Isa. 30:18 NIV)

Adam and Eve, unblemished with sin, were friends of the Father. The Lord God used to walk with them in the cool of the day (Gen. 3:8). He walked with them and talked with them face-to-face.

When Adam and Eve sinned, humanity's fellowship with God was broken. Sinful man could not stand in the presence of a holy God. It was impossible. Not even Moses was allowed to look into God's face, for to do so would mean certain death (Exod. 33:19–23).

Sin created a barrier in the relationship between God and humans. However, despite the barrier, the inclination of the Father's heart was still toward friendship. The Lord spoke to Moses "as a man speaks with his friend" (Exod. 33:11 NIV); he called Abraham "friend" (Isa. 41:8; James 2:23). King Solomon recognized him as the friend who "sticks closer than a brother" (Prov. 18:24), and the children of Israel called him, "My Father, my friend from my youth" (Jer. 3:4 NIV).

The Father's desire for fellowship and friendship with his children is most evident in the life of Jesus. Jesus called his disciples "friends." The religious leaders sarcastically called Jesus the "friend of tax collectors sinners" to criticize his friendly relationship with those who were social outcasts (Luke 7:34).

Jesus laid down his life so that we could be friends with his Father. But there are conditions to friendship with God, for friendship with God is not like human friendship. We are not God's equals, nor are we his peers. The Father longs for us to be his friends, but our friendship with him is, of necessity, on his terms. He alone knows what makes friendship between divinity and humans possible.

John 15:9–15 emphasizes several aspects of friendship with God. It tells us that Jesus demonstrated the greatness of the Father's love when he laid down his life for his friends (v. 13) and that we are friends of God if we do what he commands (v. 14). Servants do not know their Master's business, but Jesus revealed the Father's heart to us. Therefore, we are no longer called "servants," but are called friends (v. 15).

FATHER OF COMPASSION

Why would the Father want us to be his friends? It is not as though he lacks anything or would gain anything by our friendship

(Acts 17:25). What is his motivation? We find an answer in 2 Corinthians 1:3. Paul refers to God as "the Father of compassion" (NIV).

Compassion is a tender emotion that arises from observing the unfortunate circumstances of another, accompanied by a desire to help and be involved. The Father wants to be our friend not because it will benefit him but because he is a God of compassion. He sees our circumstance, and he is moved with tender emotion. According to Psalm 78:39, he remembers that we are "but flesh." Therefore, he wants to help us and be involved in our lives.

Compassion, like love and kindness, is a defining characteristic of the Father's personality. David often coupled this characteristic of compassion with "graciousness." The Lord is "gracious and compassionate" (Ps. 111:4 NIV; see also 86:15; 103:8; 145:8).

To be "gracious" means to be characterized by benevolence. It is a desire to promote the well-being and happiness of others. That describes the Father's basic attitude toward you. He has a predisposition toward your well-being. You never have to wonder whether the Father wants the best for you. The Father is gracious and full of compassion. He is the Father of compassion.

THE FATHER IS MOVED BY YOU

In my mind I can still see my oldest son sitting on the floor in the entrance of our home, trying to tie his own shoes. He was just four years old, and he couldn't coordinate his chubby little fingers to get the strings right. I remember watching from around the corner. He tried and tried again and finally threw himself down on the floor in tears, frustration, and anger.

I was moved with compassion. I saw that he was unable to do the task, and I wanted to help. Psalm 103:13 says that the Father has compassion toward us in the same way. "As a father has compassion on his children, so the LORD has compassion on those who fear him; for he knows how we are formed, he remembers that we are dust" (Ps. 103:13–14 NIV).

Have you ever considered that your heavenly Father is moved with compassion for you? He sees and knows that you are not big enough for the task, and he is right there, wanting to help and be involved. His heart is tender toward you. "Yet the Lord longs to be

gracious to you; He rises to show you compassion" (Isa. 30:18 NIV).
That means:

- The Father has tender feelings toward you.
- The Father is concerned with what is happening in your
life.
- The Father wants to be involved in your life.
- The Father is moved by you, rising to show you compassion.

In grade school, when I wanted to remember something important, I would write a note on the palm of my hand with ink. The
inscription was always in front of me. I could not help but take notice
and remember.

The Father says to you, "See, I have inscribed you on the palms
of My hands; Your walls are continually before Me" (Isa. 49:16). God
has permanently inscribed you on the palms of his hands. You are continually before him, in his thoughts and the stirrings of his heart. To
him you are infinitely important.

Let me suggest an exercise to remind you of this passage. Write
the reference "Isaiah 49:16" on the palms of your hands clearly with a
ballpoint pen. Don't wash the ink off until evening. Each time you
notice the writing on your palms, think of how you are inscribed on
the palms of the Father's hands and how you are continually before
him.

THE FATHER IS RELATIONSHIP ORIENTED

We have been looking at the characteristics of the Father's heart.
The Father loves you; he wants to crown you with his love. The Father
is kind and gentle. The Father is always with you. He wants to be your
friend. These characteristics show that the Father is relationship ori-
ented and that he wants to be in relationship with you.

Maria had always felt that God the Father was distant and did not
think a close relationship with him was possible. After doing the *In
My Father's House* Bible study, she exclaimed, "Now I'm 'glued' to my
heavenly Father. I'm sitting on his knee, dining with him, and getting
to know him better!"

Would you like to experience a closer relationship with God the
Father? Let me ask you to end this chapter by praying the following
prayer, which is based on Ephesians 1:17:

"Dear God of my Lord Jesus Christ, most glorious Father, give me the Spirit of wisdom and revelation, so that I may know you better. Enlighten the eyes of my heart. Crown me with your love. Help me to draw near. I want to be your friend. Amen."

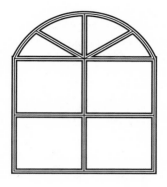

P A R T   3

Getting to Know God
as Father:
Father God Looks
after You

The eyes of the LORD are on the righteous,
And His ears are open to their cry. . . .
The righteous cry out, and the LORD hears,
And delivers them out of all their troubles.
The LORD is near to those who have a broken heart,
And saves such as have a contrite spirit.
Many are the afflictions of the righteous,
But the LORD delivers him out of them all.

—PSALM 34:15, 17–19

To question God's goodness is not just an intellectual experiment. It is a little child with tears in its eyes looking up at Daddy and weeping, "Why?" It is the question put to the Father, not a question asked in a vacuum.

The hurt child needs not so much explanations as reassurances. And that is what we get: the reassurance of the Father in the person of Jesus, "He who has seen Me has seen the Father" (John 14:9). . . .

Henceforth, when we feel the hammers of life beating on our heads or on our hearts, we can know—we must know—that He is here with us, taking our blows. Every tear we shed becomes His tear. He may not yet wipe them away, but He makes them His. Would we rather have our own dry eyes, or His tear-filled ones? He came. He is here. That is the salient fact. If He does not heal all our broken bones and loves and lives now, He comes into them and is broken, like bread, and we are nourished.

—Peter Kreeft[1]

CHAPTER 12

FATHER GOD IS STRONG AND POWERFUL

My favorite picture of my husband is not our wedding picture. It is not a pic-
ture of the two of us together, nor is it one of him alone. My favorite picture
of my husband is a picture of him cuddling our newborn daughter against
his chest. His hands are big and strong; his skin rough, sunned, and hairy.
She is tiny, soft, smooth, and so seemingly vulnerable in contrast. Yet she
sleeps in perfect safety and contentment with her downy head cradled in the
crook of his neck.

There is something powerful about the picture. It captures something
about my husband's maleness and something about his character that is dif-
ficult to express. It is something that is attractive to me. He is strong, muscu-
lar, and self-sufficient. But the look on his face reflects compassion and
commitment. His eyes are set with resolve to protect, nurture, and strengthen
the little child in his arms. His strength and capability stand in marked con-
trast to her weakness and vulnerability. But he is bound by honor and by
love to use his great strength to serve her. He will be her rock.

This picture of my husband with our daughter reminds me of the
fatherhood of God. When I think of my heavenly Father, I think of safety,
stability, strength, and security. Father God is strong and powerful. He is my
refuge, my strength. He is my Father. He is my rock.

—Becky

The LORD reigns, He is clothed with majesty;
The LORD is clothed,
He has girded Himself with strength. (Ps. 93:1)

My hand will sustain him;
surely my arm will strengthen him. . . .
He will call out to me, "You are my Father,
my God, the Rock my Savior." (Ps. 89:21, 26 NIV)

Ascribe strength to God;
His excellence is over Israel,
And His strength is in the clouds.
O God, You are more awesome than Your holy places.
The God of Israel is He who gives strength and power
    to His people. (Ps. 68:34–35)

Have you not known?
Have you not heard?
The everlasting God, the LORD,
The Creator of the ends of the earth,
Neither faints nor is weary.
There is no searching of His understanding.
He gives power to the weak,
And to those who have no might He increases strength.
(Isa. 40:28–29)

"Blessed are You, LORD God of Israel, our Father, forever
    and ever.
Yours, O LORD, is the greatness,
The power and the glory,
The victory and the majesty; . . .
In Your hand is power and might;
In Your hand it is to make great
And to give strength to all." (1 Chron. 29:10–12)

The LORD is my strength and my shield; . . . My heart leaps
for joy . . . The LORD is the strength of His people.
(Ps. 28:7–9 NIV)

This morning at the breakfast table, I reminded my children that
their father's two-year term as president of his professional college
would soon be ending. "That's too bad," sighed my son Matthew.
"I really liked telling all my friends that Dad was the president."

Children love to brag about their fathers. Rare is the child who has not boasted about his or her father's abilities. "My dad is so smart." "My dad can run fast." "My dad is strong."

Our heavenly Father is strong and powerful. One of his names, *Yahweh Sabaoth* reflects that fact. *Sabaoth* means "almighty." Might is the ability or power to do or accomplish. It means effective power and strength.

In Psalm 68:34, David tells us to "ascribe strength" to God. Likewise, in Psalm 29:1, David encourages us to "ascribe . . . glory and strength" to him (NIV). To *ascribe* means "to attribute to; to give credit." Ascribing strength to the Father means that we see and acknowledge his great strength and mighty power.

David delighted in God the Father's strength in much the same manner as my children boast about how strong their dad is. "Who is mighty like You, O LORD? . . . You have a mighty arm; strong is Your hand, and high is Your right hand" (Ps. 89:8, 13). "The LORD is robed in majesty and is armed with strength" (Ps. 93:1 NIV).

In the Psalms, David often reflected upon the great strength of the Lord. He saw God's strength evident in all creation: wild and domestic animals, thunderous waterfalls, towering forests, expansive deserts, lofty mountains, stars. But David also saw the strength of God in the fearful destructive power of floods, tornadoes, earthquakes, fire, hurricanes, fierce lightning, and thunder. According to David, the Father is so strong that the mere sound of his voice can initiate massive natural devastation. The following paraphrase from the Living Bible illustrates how strong God the Father is:

Praise the Lord, you angels of his; praise his glory and his strength. . . .

The voice of the Lord echoes from the clouds. The God of glory thunders through the skies. So powerful is his voice; so full of majesty. It breaks down the cedars. It splits the giant trees of Lebanon. It shakes Mount Lebanon and Mount Sirion. They leap and skip before him like young calves! The voice of the Lord thunders through the lightning. It resounds through the deserts and shakes the wilderness of Kadesh. The voice of the Lord spins and topples the mighty oaks. It strips the forests bare. They whirl and sway beneath the blast. But in his temple all are praising, "Glory, glory to the Lord."

At the Flood, the Lord showed his control of all creation. Now he continues to unveil his power. He will give his people strength. He will bless them with peace. (Ps. 29:1, 3–11 TLB)

The natural evidences of the strength and power of God cited in this passage are awesome and perhaps even frightening. We must agree with Jeremiah, who said, "Ah, Lord GOD! Behold, You have made the heavens and the earth by Your great power and outstretched arm. There is nothing too hard for You" (Jer. 32:17).

The Father's Strength to Help His Children

My father was a carpenter. I used to love sitting in his workshop watching him make wonderful things out of wood. As a girl the thing that impressed me the most was the size and strength of his hands. Dad's hands were large and strong. They were also skilled. Dad could make, fix, open, twist, pry, bend, or straighten almost anything in the world.

Dad's strength was not merely a trait to be admired. As children (and even as grown children) we benefited from it in practical ways. Dad used his strength and skill to serve us. Whenever there was a task too difficult for us, we would run to our father for help. The phrase my dad undoubtedly heard the most in his lifetime was, "Dad, could you please help me?"

My Dad's display of strength was different from the strength displayed at Mr. World-type competitions where men with oil-slicked, steroid-pumped bodies pose in every which way to show off their muscles. Mr. World men want us to admire them, stroke their egos, and give them a prize. Their strength is self-serving.

My Dad did not hide his strength. I knew that he was strong. But this was not pride on his part. It was not self-serving. On the contrary, Dad wanted us to be aware of his strength so that we would know we could rely on him and go to him for help. His strength was focused on helping others.

Father God acts in the same way. He uses his great strength to serve and help us. Father God does not flex his muscles so we will stroke his ego. Nor does he use his strength to abuse and humiliate. No. He wants us to recognize his great power and strength so that we might trust in him, rely on him, and go to him for help.

King David gave us a profound insight in Psalm 68:35. He tells us what God likes to do with his strength and power: "You are awesome, O God, in your sanctuary; the God of Israel gives power and strength to his people. Praise be to God!" (NIV).

Did you notice that God does not give aid only to prophets, leaders, and teachers? He doesn't give strength only to those who are perfect. Our Father God gives his power to all of his children.

THE FATHER'S STRENGTH, SOURCE OF MANY BLESSINGS

The strength of the Father is available to all of his children. The Father's strength is the source of many blessings. It is a source of help and strength. It is also a source of peace and security, safety and refuge. We can be confident and sure-footed because of the Father's strength. It gives us great joy.

Psalm 28:7 states the principle in powerful words:

The LORD is my strength and my shield; my heart trusts in him, and I am helped. My heart leaps for joy and I will give thanks to him in song.

Based on the words of the psalm we can see that David believed—
• The Father makes me strong.
• I can trust the Father with all my heart.
• The Father will help me.

I don't have to live depending on my own self-sufficiency. I am sadly mistaken when I think I can't rely on the Father for help.

Peace and Security

The passage in Psalm 29 that we studied at the beginning of this chapter speaks of the awesome strength of God as witnessed in natural disasters. How the passage ends has great significance for us. If you look back to the last two sentences, you will read that the Lord gives his people strength and blesses them with peace.

David was not afraid of the awesome strength of God. On the contrary, he regarded it as the source of his own strength. He also regarded it as a source of blessing and peace. In 2 Samuel 22:3, David calls God his stronghold. A stronghold is a fortified place, a place of security. The mighty strength of God gave David peace and made him feel secure.

Consider the awesome strength of God the Father. Does his strength frighten you, or does it give you peace and security? Some people feel totally intimidated and frightened when they think about the strength of the Father. Others derive a great feeling of peace and security from God's dependability and strength.

I wish we could sit down over a cup of coffee and share our hearts about this key part of life. Do you sometimes feel afraid to trust God totally? Or do you delight in the Father's strength? By unpacking both the truth of Scripture and our own feelings, I believe we can learn to see and feel God's power as a source of blessing and peace.

Safety and Refuge

Some women and men fear the strength of God the Father because their earthly fathers physically or sexually harmed them. Such tragic life experiences make trusting the Father's strength much more difficult. If you have faced such pain, let me encourage you to rely on the truth of the Bible and not on your own personal experience of earthly fatherhood. The more we get to know the God of Scripture, the more we realize that his strength is never abusive. It is a source of safety and refuge for his children:

> The name of the Lord is a strong tower;
> the righteous run to it and are safe. (Prov. 18:10 NIV)

> He is my loving God and my fortress,
> my stronghold and my deliverer,
> my shield, in whom I take refuge. (Ps. 144:2 NIV)

Katie's earthly father was alcoholic and physically abusive. She lived in constant fear of his drunken rages. When she was in her teens, her father finally left. But instead of relief, Katie felt abandoned. In her heart she felt more secure with a father who was present but at times abusive than she did without the strength and protection a father offered. "I felt so weak and vulnerable," she explains, "and I craved someone to love and protect me." Sadly, the unfulfilled need in Katie's spirit caused her to be attracted to the wrong kind of men—men who, like her father, used their strength in an abusive way. It was not until she realized that her desire for a strong protector could be found in Father God that she began her journey toward wholeness. "God has become the father I never knew," she says. "He is strong, but that strength is loving, caring, and nurturing."

The Father is a strong tower. You can run to the Father and be safe. He loves you. He is your fortress, your stronghold, your deliverer, your shield. You can take refuge in his strength.

If you cannot agree to this truth right now, I pray that you will keep pursuing it, like Katie did. Don't give up or give in to a life without the security of your Father's power. Share your struggle with him. Make a commitment to try to overcome your fear. Continue to say to him: "Dear Father, give me the Spirit of wisdom and revelation, so that I may know you better" (see Eph. 1:17).

Confidence and Sure-Footedness

I live near the Canadian Rocky Mountains. Every year when we visit the national parks, we see wildlife. Often we will see deer and mountain goats scaling the side of a cliff. It is a remarkable sight. These animals are so sure-footed that they are stable on even the narrowest outcropping of rock.

David said that God's strength gave him the confidence and sure-footedness of a deer. "God is my strength and power, and He makes my way perfect. He makes my feet like the feet of deer, and sets me on my high places. . . . Your gentleness has made me great. You enlarged my path under me; so my feet did not slip" (2 Sam. 22:33–34, 36–37).

Habakkuk agreed with David. "The Lord God is my strength; He will make my feet like deer's feet, And He will make me walk on my high hills" (Hab. 3:19).

Can you identify with David's and Habakkuk's words? Have you stood on a narrow ledge in your life in need of the Father's strength? Perhaps it has been a difficult circumstance, a fractured relationship, sickness, or death. In that time were you able to benefit from his strength through your confidence in him?

I believe that many times we don't get the practical help we need from Father God's power because we don't have confidence to lean on him. I want to encourage you to develop new habits. Wouldn't it be wonderful to develop the pattern of calling on the Father to give you the confidence and sure-footedness of a deer? When you first begin to feel that tottering, unstable feeling, ask him to enlarge the path under you so your feet will not slip. Ask him to help you walk on your high hill. The Father is strong and mighty. And the Father wants to use his great strength to help you.

Joy

When my husband, Brent, was five years old, a fire broke out in the next-door neighbor's house. The family had escaped unharmed. Brent's father, who was one of the town's volunteer firefighters, joined the other men in battling the blaze. Brent remembers watching in pride as his father fought the fire and kept the flames from harming their house. He was confident that his father could extinguish the fire and keep their home safe. Though excited by all the commotion, little Brent was unafraid. His father's strength gave him confidence and joy in the midst of danger. Brent's trust in his father caused him to regard the incident as an adventure rather than a crisis.

The final blessing of the Father's strength is the blessing of joy. David took great joy in the strength of God. He wrote, "O LORD, the king rejoices in your strength. How great is his joy in the victories you give!" (Ps. 21:1 NIV). Does knowledge of the Father's strength bring you confidence and joy? Are you able to face the battles and dangers of life with a childlike faith that your heavenly Father will eventually put out the flames and all will be well? Confidence in his strength frees us from anxiety and enables us to experience great peace and joy, even in the midst of danger. It allows us to have the same "Dad is strong, he'll take care of it" attitude toward our heavenly Father that Brent had toward his earthly father.

Here are the blessings we have seen associated with the Father's strength. Which of these blessings do you need most in your life?

- Help and strength
- Peace and security
- Safety and refuge
- Confidence and sure-footedness
- Joy

King David said, "You [God] are my strength. . . . Your gentleness has made me great" (2 Sam. 22:33, 36) and "Strength and beauty are in His sanctuary" (Ps. 96:6). David associated the strength of the Father with gentleness and with beauty. The Father's strength is gentle. It is beautiful.

David encourages us to seek the Lord and his strength: "Seek the Lord and His strength; Seek His face evermore" (Ps. 105:4). In what areas of your life do you need help? In these areas, are you seeking the face of the Father? Are you relying on his strength?

In this chapter we have explored some powerful truths. Some of us have more trouble than others embracing these realities. I want to encourage you that these foundation stones can stabilize your life. Write them down. Meditate on them. Make them yours.

- The Father's strength is powerful and mighty. It is also gentle and beautiful.
- Nothing is too hard for him.
- Your heavenly Father wants to use his great strength to help you. You can call on him for help in all areas of life.
- As you seek the strength of your heavenly Father, you will receive blessings of help, strength, peace, security, safety, and refuge. You will be confident and sure-footed. His strength will be a source of great joy.

CHAPTER 13

FATHER GOD IS PROTECTIVE

When I think about my childhood, I remember only one loving, pure cuddle from my Father. The following years of childhood and adolescence are blurred by the pain of abuse, both physical and sexual. As a young woman, I blamed myself. I felt unclean and unworthy of being loved. I searched and searched for love and acceptance only to be used and hurt again and again. Then I met my Savior, Jesus. To me, Jesus was a trusted friend. Over the years Jesus gently led me to his Father. I longed for a daddy to care for me, but I was so afraid. Old fears blocked the way. I mentally struggled with searing memories. But little by little deep healing came. Over and over again I heard the Father speak words of gentle love, "I have loved you with an everlasting love, you are mine, I have paid the ultimate price for you. . . . I will not harm you." As he caressed me with his gentle, loving words, my heart started to respond, and I began to trust him. One day in prayer I saw myself sitting on my Father's lap. Looking into his face, I threw my arms open wide, and he held me close. "Daddy," I whispered. The words came from my lips and my heart. I knew that finally the pain of the past was over, engulfed in the rapture of this moment that would go on forever. My perception of my heavenly Father is complete now. He is everything I have ever dreamt of. Truly he is my Abba Father, "Daddy God" who loves, protects, and treasures me as his special girl.

—Emily

He will cover you with his feathers,
   and under his wings you will find refuge;
   his faithfulness will be your shield and rampart.
(Ps. 91:4 NIV)

Have mercy on me, O God, have mercy on me,
for in you my soul takes refuge.
I will take refuge in the shadow of your wings
until the disaster has passed.
I cry out to God Most High,
to God, who fulfills his purpose for me.
He sends from heaven and saves me. . . . God sends his love
and his faithfulness. (Ps. 57:1–3 NIV)

The women I spoke with who had good relationships with their earthly fathers almost always mentioned that they felt protected by their dads.

"With Dad, I always felt very safe."

"Dad gave me a sense of security."

"Dad would make sure nothing harmed me."

"Dad always protected me."

"I was confident that my dad would look out for me and protect me."

"Dad was my gentle guardian warrior."

"I knew that if anyone ever hurt me, he would have to answer to my dad."

John Piper believes that a sense of "responsibility to protect" is one of the primary traits that characterizes mature masculinity.[1] Mothers also protect and guard their children, particularly in the absence of a father or a father figure. However, in an intact, healthy family, the responsibility to protect the family appears to fall primarily on the father. Think of your childhood. How safe and protected did you feel as a child? Did you feel safe or vulnerable to being harmed? Why do you think you felt this way? Was your father there for you? Or did you have someone else who protected you? Were there events in your life that made you feel vulnerable?

Protecting our children is a prime characteristic of responsible fathering.

We humans inherited the characteristic from the fatherhood of God. Notice the words and phrases in these passages that demonstrate how the Father protects his children:

I will rescue him;
I will protect him, for he acknowledges my name.
He will call upon me, and I will answer him;
I will be with him in trouble,
I will deliver him and honor him. (Ps. 91:14–15 NIV)

May the LORD answer you when you are in distress;
may the name of the God of Jacob protect you.
May he send you help from the sanctuary
and grant you support from Zion. (Ps. 20:1–2 NIV)

He said, "Surely they are my people,
sons who will not be false to me",
and so he became their Savior.
In all their distress he too was distressed,
and the angel of his presence saved them.
In his love and mercy he redeemed them;
he lifted them up and carried them
all the days of old. (Isa. 63:8–9 NIV)

Fear not, for I have redeemed you;
I have summoned you by name; you are mine.
When you pass through the waters,
I will be with you;
and when you pass through the rivers,
they will not sweep over you.
When you walk through the fire,
you will not be burned;
the flames will not set you ablaze. (Isa. 43:1–2 NIV)

Because I had an earthly father who always protected me and because I was not abused by any of the men in my life, it is easy for me to believe the Scriptures and to trust in the protection of my heavenly Father.

But what about those who have experienced physical and sexual abuse, sometimes at the hands of the fathers who should have been their protectors? How does that influence their trust in God the Father? And why does the heavenly Father allow such things to happen to his children? How can he be their protector if he does not protect them from abuse?

These difficult questions haunt many women, and many women reject the fatherhood of God because of them. Emily, whose story you read at the beginning of this chapter, came to know Jesus after years of incest and physical abuse. It was difficult for her to draw near to the Father. But as she got to know the Father, her trust began to grow.

Unlike Emily, Grace was raised in a Christian home. She committed her life to Jesus at a young age and was always part of a Christian community. She knew and trusted God the Father when the abuse began. Grace was severely and repeatedly sexually abused for a number of years, beginning at age ten.

The remainder of the chapter records my conversation with Grace. Hers is a powerful story. I relate it to you so that you can understand more about the protection of Father God from the perspective of someone who has suffered terrible abuse.

Mary: Grace, you were terribly abused when you were young. Did you call out to God the Father during that time?

Grace: Yes, I did. I prayed and prayed and pleaded for him to stop the nightmare of what was happening.

Mary: And did he answer?

Grace: I did not feel at the time that he did. I felt as though he sat back and never did a thing about it. My trust in him was shattered. I was really angry. I thought, *A friend doesn't stand by and let a friend get hurt like that! Why, if he was my loving Father, didn't he intervene?* I felt like God didn't care. I felt that he wasn't actively participating in my life. I felt as though he was watching me like he'd watch a movie: indifferent, or perhaps even enjoying my pain.

Mary: After the abuse stopped, did things get better?

Grace: No. Things got even worse. I was filled with anger, bitterness, hatred, fear, and shame. I felt I had a right to be angry and bitter. My life became black and dark. Over the following years I became obsessive-compulsive, taking three to four showers a day to try to feel clean. I became a control and cleanliness freak. I was anorexic and then bulimic. I spent months in a psychiatric ward. I still was involved in church but angry at God and at my abusers. Everything in me wanted to scream: "Go to hell! You deserve it!"

Mary: What happened to turn things around?

Grace: I hit rock bottom. I realized that the things I thought I was controlling, my eating and my environment, were really controlling me. I would cut myself with razors and not feel it. I tried to commit suicide.

At that point—at the darkest, blackest point—I looked back to God. I had nothing else. There was nothing else and no one else who was able to help me. I had tried everything: the church, pastors, psychiatrists, friends. There was no hope in anything else. So I said, "God, I don't even really like you right now. I don't trust you. But I will choose to give you what I've got. I give up. I am tired. I choose to trust you. I choose to believe that what you say is true. You are my only hope."

God took that. It was enough for him. He took it and blessed it and began to heal me.

Mary: Tell me about the healing process.

Grace: It wasn't easy. I continually had to choose to trust God. I had to stop running, look directly at my pain and my hatred, and then I had to choose to believe truth.

God gave me a picture in my mind. It was a picture of Jesus kneeling next to me beside a treasure chest that represented my heart. We opened the chest. It was filled with ugly, dark, horrible things—hatred, resentment, bitterness, wrong thinking about God. I reached into the chest and picked up an object. At that moment I had a choice. I could hang on to the ugly object and put it back in the chest, or I could give it to Jesus. It was really difficult to give up the darkness. It was what I knew, what I was familiar with. But each time I did, Jesus gave me a precious, shining jewel in return. The jewel was a portion of joy, peace, contentment, or the Father's love. This process continued over a number of years. Each time I had a dark feeling or thought, I had the choice to give it up or to hang on to it. As I surrendered, healing came.

During this process I had to learn to forgive my abusers. I do not mean to say that I will ever condone what they did. It was wrong, and it was evil. But I had to release all the bitterness, hatred, vengeance, and my right to retribution. For me to be free, I had to give it all to Jesus.

Mary: Did your circumstances improve?

Grace: Not all of them and not immediately. I went through a relationship with an abusive boyfriend, experimented with drugs, and was married for a short time to an abusive man who claimed to be a Christian. I did not always make good decisions. Now I am struggling with being a single mom. But through it all, God is faithful.

Mary: What do you think about the abuse now? Where was God?

Grace: God was there.

I don't know why, but God allows people free will. Even people who abuse others. Abuse was not what he had planned or wanted for me. He wanted beauty for me. So he took something as evil and ugly as abuse and made beauty out of it. God the Father saw the big picture. He was there. At the time I didn't think he was, but now I know he was there.

Mary: So do you believe that God the Father is your protector? And if so, what does that mean?

Grace: Hmm. Yes. Yes, I would say that the Father is my protector. But that does not mean that people will never hurt me. I guess I have a different understanding of protection than I used to.

It's so easy to ask, "Why didn't God protect me?" A better question might be, "What did God protect me from?"

In looking at my situation now, I see that God did protect me. I could have become pregnant, but I didn't. My abuser vowed to kill me, but he didn't. The abuse could have gone on for many more years, but it didn't. I could have died in bitterness and rebellion against God, but I didn't. Now I keep thinking, *If God had not been with me, it could have been worse, much worse.*

To me the Father's protection means that nothing is going to happen to me that he is unaware of and that he will not be able to help me through or help me heal from. He is with me. He won't leave me. That doesn't mean that I will never be harmed. But it does mean that nothing will happen to me that doesn't go past the cross first. The Father has promised that no one can take Jesus away from me. Ultimately, no matter what happens to me in this world, I will have Jesus. Now that's protection!

Protection means that the Father will be with me through everything. It means that after every trial he will pick me up, dust me off, help me get over it, and send me on my way again as a better and stronger person.

Mary: So would you say that "all things work together for good"?

Grace: (laughing) I used to hate that verse! My Christian friends would glibly quote it to me without any idea of the pain and agony of the struggle. But now I see that the wisest and most godly people I know are people who have gone through the deepest valleys. They understand pain.

I can honestly say that I would never go back and change anything that happened to me. It was awful, but the experience revealed the Father's love for me. I can see now that I was important enough to him to stick by me through it all.

If he had taken me right out of the situation or healed me instantly, I would have been spoiled. I would have never appreciated what he did for me. I had to go through the struggle for him to prove his love for me. At first I thought he allowed my heart to be broken because he didn't care. Now I see that my experiences allowed God to show me how much he did care. The bigness of the struggle showed me the bigness of his love.

After you've been in the fire for so long, you either burn up or you become refined. He is refining me to be a beautiful jewel. I know with certainty and with confidence that God is on the throne and that he is standing with me and that I am his beloved daughter. I wouldn't go back and give that up for anything in the world.

Now, in my struggles, I say: "God, take it all; just don't leave me. All I need is you. No matter how bad it is, I've got hope if I've got you. No matter how quiet you are, I've got hope because I know you're there."

Mary: How do you feel about the future?

Grace: I have contentment and hope and a great love for Jesus, more than I would have ever thought possible. And I feel as though God is restoring the years the locusts have eaten. My past doesn't look all that great, but I'm sure excited about what he's going to do in the future.

Mary: What advice would you give to someone who is having difficulty trusting the Father?

Grace: Don't base your trust on experience. Base it on the truth of God's Word. And don't let go. Don't ever let go of God. Read the Word. Pray. Choose to believe truth. Feed your mind with truth. The truth is what sets you free.

And I'd tell anyone in the situation to get help and godly counsel when necessary. Do not give up. Do not lose hope. God is faithful. I know without a doubt that he will help you.

Has Grace's story helped you understand more about the protection of the Father? Look again at the words of Isaiah:

> But now, this is what the LORD says—
> he who created you, O Jacob,
> he who formed you, O Israel:
> "Fear not, for I have redeemed you;
> I have summoned you by name; you are mine.
> When you pass through the waters,
> I will be with you;
> and when you pass through the rivers,
> they will not sweep over you.
> When you walk through the fire,
> you will not be burned;
> the flames will not set you ablaze.
> For I am the LORD, your God,
> the Holy One of Israel, your Savior;
> I give Egypt for your ransom,
> Cush and Seba in your stead." (Isa. 43:1–3 NIV)

As Grace said, abuse is not what the Father has planned or wants for his children. If you are currently being abused, please get help. The biblical precedent for abusive situations is fleeing to safety. You need to get help. You need to remove yourself from danger into a position of safety in order to heal and to allow the situation to be effectively addressed and hopefully redeemed.

For those who are struggling with the aftereffects of past abuse, remember Grace's words: "At first I thought he allowed my heart to be broken because he didn't care. Now I see that he allowed it to show me how much he did care. *The bigness of the struggle showed me the bigness of his love.*"

Father God loved Grace so much that he walked with her through every step of the healing process. In the end, what she gained on the journey was infinitely greater and more precious than what she had suffered and lost.

As Peter Kreeft said in the quote at the beginning of this section:

Henceforth, when we feel the hammers of life beating on our
heads or on our hearts, we can know—we must know—that
He is here with us, taking our blows. Every tear we shed
becomes His tear. He may not yet wipe them away, but He
makes them His. Would we rather have our own dry eyes, or
His tear-filled ones? He came. He is here. That is the salient
fact. If He does not heal all our broken bones and loves and
lives now, He comes into them and is broken, like bread, and
we are nourished.

CHAPTER 14

PRINCIPLES OF THE FATHER'S PROTECTION

My dad had all sorts of rules. No dating till I was sixteen. No going to school dances. As a child I did not always agree with his decisions, and I sometimes felt that he did not understand my point of view. I had one boyfriend whom Dad totally disapproved of. He did not forbid me from seeing the boy, but he definitely let me know how he felt about the relationship. As an adult looking back at these things, I realize that my dad made decisions to protect me from dangers and lead me to growth that I could not see. He always had and still has his girl's best interest at heart. When I think of how my earthly father loved and protected me, I have a wonderful sense of security in God the Father. As much as my dad loves me, God loves me infinitely more. If my dad did what was best for me, how much more will my heavenly Father protect me and lead me where he knows it is best? Because I could trust my earthly father, I now find it easy to trust my heavenly Father.

—Renate

Fear not, for I have redeemed you;
I have summoned you by name; you are mine.
When you pass through the waters,
I will be with you;
and when you pass through the rivers,
they will not sweep over you.

When you walk through the fire,
you will not be burned;
the flames will not set you ablaze. (Isa. 43:1–3 NIV)

But let all who take refuge in you be glad;
let them ever sing for joy.
Spread your protection over them,
that those who love your name may rejoice in you.
For surely, O LORD, you bless the righteous;
you surround them with your favor as with a shield.
(Ps. 5:11–12 NIV)

If you have ever been to Niagara Falls, you know that the water crashes down over a staggering precipice. Under the falls, between the falling sheet of water and the face of the rock, is a vacant space called the Cave of the Winds. Tourists can robe in bright yellow rain gear and make their way along the rocks to reach this cave. At the stopping point thousands of tons of water from overhead smash with a thunderous roar just a few yards in front of where tourists stand. The splash of the spray and mist are blinding, and a strong current of air howls past each observer's face.

Imagine a father taking his young daughter on this path. She looks at him dubiously as he buttons her yellow rain gear. She becomes more and more frightened, clinging to his hand as he leads her closer to the falls and she hears the thunderous roar increase. As they draw near, the spray stings her face, and the mist becomes so thick she can no longer see.

Under the falls it is too loud to hear her father's reassuring voice. She cries out, but her tiny voice seems lost in the deafening chaos. Terrified, she screams, "Daddy!" The father scoops his frightened daughter into his arms and carries her under the remainder of the falls through to the other side.

She is chilled and soaked with water but is relieved because the danger has now passed. As they exit the tour, she points to the falls and proudly tells the gatekeeper, "My dad took me under there!"

While the danger of the falls is very real—the savage impact of the water could crush a victim to death in an instant—the little girl was safe all along. Perhaps she became wet and cold through her ordeal, and perhaps she could have slipped on a wet rock and scraped her knee, but she was not ever in danger of being significantly harmed. Not as long as she stayed close to her father. Her father could see the way. He was there to hold her hand and guide her along the safe path.

Why did he take her there? He knew the majesty and the beauty of the falls and of the cave. He knew that his daughter would get wet and would probably be frightened, but he understood what could be gained by going to the underside of the falls and seeing them from that perspective. He knew that she would be wiser for the experience.

It is the same way with the protection of God the Father. The Father is our protector. But that does not mean that he will lead us down a danger-free path. It does not mean that we will never be frightened—that we will never get cold, wet, or scrape our knees.

In this chapter we will look at some principles regarding the protection of the Father. I hope you will learn that the Father sees everything that happens to you, including your hardships, trials, and afflictions. You will also learn that the Father cares about what happens to you, that he is with you continually to uphold you and that he will supply you the strength to deal with whatever he allows you to face.

PRINCIPLE 1. THE FATHER SEES

The first principle regarding the protection of the Father is that the Father sees what is happening to you. Proverbs 15:3 says that "the eyes of the LORD are in every place." His eyes "behold" and "observe" all that takes place (Ps. 11:4; 66:7). David asked, "He who planted the ear, shall He not hear? He who formed the eye, shall He not see?" (Ps. 94:9).

The wicked sometimes think that "God has forgotten; He hides His face; He will never see" (Ps 10:11). But those who are righteous know that the Father sees everything.

Sarai, Abram's wife, had borne no children, so she encouraged Abram to sleep with her Egyptian maidservant, Hagar. When Hagar became pregnant with Abram's child, the relationship between the two women deteriorated, and Sarai began to resent and mistreat Hagar. Sarai's treatment of Hagar became so harsh and abusive that pregnant Hagar fled into the desert, intending to run away forever.

The angel of the Lord appeared to her there beside a well of water. The Lord told her that she would give birth to a son and that she was to name him Ishmael, which means "God hears," "for the LORD has heard of your misery" (Gen. 16:1–12 NIV).

Genesis 16:13 tells us the name Hagar gave to the Lord: "She gave this name to the LORD who spoke to her: 'You are the God who sees me,' for she said, 'I have now seen the One who sees me.'"

Hagar was a foreigner. She knew the loneliness of not being accepted and not fitting in. She experienced hardship and abuse as a slave. She was the illegitimate, unloved "slave wife." Even though she had produced a surrogate son for them, her mistress regarded her with ingratitude and hostility and her master with indifference and rejection. Ultimately, she and her son were dispossessed and driven away from their home (Gen. 21:8–20).

Hagar faced loneliness, pain, heartache, and at one point, certain death. But through all her trials, God was watching. The Father is the "One who sees" (Gen. 16:13 NIV).

PRINCIPLE 2. THE FATHER CARES

You probably believe that God sees when you are in danger or distress. But like Grace, at the beginning of her journey, you may not think that he really cares about your troubles.

The Bible teaches that the Father does care when he sees his children in danger or distress. The children of Israel suffered terrible affliction during their time of slavery in Egypt. God saw their suffering. Exodus 2:25 records that he looked on them and was "concerned about them" (NIV). In Hosea 11:8, the Father looks on the children of Israel when they are under siege from their enemies and laments, "My heart churns within Me; My sympathy is stirred" (NIV).

Look at the words of Isaiah that indicate how the Father is concerned when his children are in danger or distress:

> He said, "Surely they are my people,
> sons who will not be false to me";
> and so he became their Savior.
> In all their distress he too was distressed,
> and the angel of his presence saved them.
> In his love and mercy he redeemed them;
> he lifted them up and carried them
> all the days of old. (Isa. 63:8–9 NIV)

Have you ever thought that God had such an attitude? "In all their distress he too was distressed" pictures for us how the Father cares and is concerned when he sees your difficulties. Every time you are distressed, he too is distressed. When you weep, he weeps. When you hurt, he hurts.

PRINCIPLE 3. THE FATHER WILL CONTINUALLY UPHOLD YOU

About three months after the children of Israel had come out of Egypt, they were camped in the wilderness of Sinai, beside the mountain of Sinai. There, God told Moses, "You have seen what I did to the Egyptians, and how I bore you on eagles' wings and brought you to Myself" (Exod. 19:4).

Eagles are large, powerful birds. They build their eyries (nests) in the tops of tall trees or cliffs. To teach a young eaglet to fly, the parent will coax it to come out on a limb and then will push it off. Failing this, the parent will stir the nest and throw the eaglet out. The eaglet, not yet knowing how to fly, hopelessly plunges downward. The parent quickly swoops down under the eaglet and flaps its powerful wings. The eaglet does not see the parent, but the updraft of air created by the parent's wings pushes the little eaglet up, enabling it to fly.

The Father bore the Israelites "on eagles' wings." They did not see his support when they were suffering under their increased load (Exod. 5:20–22). Nor did they see him when they felt they would die, trapped by the Egyptian army, or from hunger in the desert (Exod. 14:10–12; 16:3). But the Father was continually upholding them. Like an eagle unseen, he was supporting them with his strength and his power, enabling them to fly.

Can you think of a time when your earthly father was like an eagle, supporting and protecting you "behind the scenes"? Or how about your heavenly Father? Can you think of a time when he bore you on eagle's wings? Read what the Father said through the prophet Isaiah:

Listen to Me, O house of Jacob,
And all the remnant of the house of Israel,
Who have been upheld by Me from birth,

Who have been carried from the womb:
Even to your old age, I am He
And even to gray hairs I will carry you!
I have made, and I will bear;
Even I will carry, and will deliver you. (Isa. 46:3)

Did you take note of how long the Father promised to support his children? Go back and read the verse again, looking for every action of the Father (you are looking for the verbs). The first word you will note is *upheld.* The Father upholds you from the time you are born until the time you are old. Even if you do not perceive his presence, he is bearing you on eagle's wings, enabling you to fly.

PRINCIPLE 4. THE FATHER WILL SUPPLY THE STRENGTH YOU NEED

Job was a wealthy, successful man. He was the greatest man among all the people of the East (Job 1:3). According to the Bible, Satan requested permission to inflict suffering upon Job in expectation that Job would turn against God.

God gave Satan permission to strike everything Job had but not to touch Job (1:12). Job lost all of his herds and crops, and all of his children. In spite of all this, Job did not reject God. Satan approached God a second time to ask for permission to afflict Job's body. God allowed this but disallowed Satan from taking Job's life (2:6).

Each time Satan approached God, God specified a boundary. In essence he allowed Satan to go so far but no further. God would not allow Satan to exceed that boundary.

At the end of Moses' life, he blessed the tribes of Israel. His blessings carry the weight of prophecy and promise. To the tribe of Asher, he gave a promise that I firmly believe is basic to God's character. He said, "Your strength will equal your days." This is the other side of God's limits on evil. We cannot say God will not take us through times of trial and suffering. God often prioritizes our character development over our comfort. We can guarantee, however, that God will limit the burdens and temptations that come our way, and he'll supply strength to equal our days. This is the fourth principle of the Father's protection. We need not fear, for we belong to the Father, and he ensures that we will be able to bear whatever we go through.

In the last chapter we looked at Isaiah 43:1–2. Verse 2 tells us how the Father ensures that we will be able to bear the difficulties we encounter: "When you pass through the waters, I will be with you; and when you pass through the rivers, they will not sweep over you. When you walk through the fire, you will not be burned; the flames will not set you ablaze" (NIV).

The Father is with you through every difficulty and every trial. He is your helper, your friend, and your protector. He draws boundaries around what Satan is able to do to you. You may not see him at the time, but when the trial is over, you can—like the little girl at Niagara Falls—point back to the cave under the falls and say with pride, "My Father took me under there!" Or like Grace you can say, "The bigness of the struggle proved the bigness of his love!"

You can pray Isaiah 43:1–3 back to the Father. You might pray something like this:

Father, you have summoned me by name; I am yours. I will not fear, for you have redeemed me. When I pass through the waters, You will be with me; and when I pass through the rivers, they will not sweep over me. When I walk through the fire, I will not be burned; the flames will not set me ablaze; for You are with me. You are my helper and protector. You are my loving Father.

CHAPTER 15

MORE PRINCIPLES OF THE FATHER'S PROTECTION

As a father, I believe one of the most important things I bring to my family is my desire and ability to protect them. Physically, I am stronger than they. When threatened, the adrenaline rushes, and I instinctively put myself between them and danger. In my family, I am the guy who will take the bullet.

I remember one time when an older boy maliciously knocked my daughter off of her bike and rode off with it. I bolted down the street; my wife followed. I could hear her muttering niceties about contacting the parents and talking to the boy. All I could think of was catching him and taking him to the wall. If there weren't laws against it, I would have turned that boy over then and there and spanked him.

But the protection I offer is more than physical. I think protection also involves mental and spiritual preparation. Protecting my children means safeguarding them not only against physical harm but also against moral and spiritual harm. I protect my children by preparing them for the dangers that life is going to throw their way. I protect my daughter by exemplifying for her what a good man is and by teaching her to respect herself and to stay away from men that will harm her. I am her example and her backup. I protect my son by training him to stand strong against pressure. I protect him by training him to be a man of strength, virtue, and honor.

Protection means keeping my children from physical harm. But it also means teaching them a way of living. As a father, it is one of my main responsibilities.

—Mike

Have mercy on me, O God, have mercy on me,
for in you my soul takes refuge.
I will take refuge in the shadow of your wings
until the disaster has passed.
I cry out to God Most High,
to God, who fulfills his purpose for me.
He sends from heaven and saves me. . . .
God sends his love and his faithfulness. (Ps. 57:1–3 NIV)

But may the God of all grace, who called us to His eternal
glory by Christ Jesus, after you have suffered a while, perfect,
establish, strengthen, and settle you. (1 Pet. 5:10)

You let men ride over our heads;
we went through fire and water,
but you brought us to a place of abundance.
(Ps. 66:12 NIV)

Those who know your name will trust in you,
for you, LORD, have never forsaken those who seek you.
(Ps. 9:10 NIV)

When my youngest son, Jonathan, was seven, he proudly presented me with a large pencil drawing. The picture showed a stick man standing on a pier, a stick dog at his side. The sky was dark with clouds and covered with streaks of heavy rain. Four stick figures were being tossed about in the huge waves. These figures were calling out for help. The stick man on the pier was shouting, "Here I come!"

I asked Jonathan to explain the picture to me. "Well," he said, "that's Daddy on the pier, and that's us in the water. Daddy is coming to save us because that's what dads are for."

I put the picture in my box of special things. To me it beautifully illustrates the simple faith of a child who unconditionally trusts his father. Dad is his protector. The fact that I am a better swimmer never even entered Jonathan's mind. "Dad will save us. That's what dads are for."

Let's look at the remaining three principles of the Father's protection. Our heavenly Father, like the stick father in Jonathan's picture, says, "I'm here. I'm coming!" He will protect and deliver us. That, according to the Bible, is what the Father is for.

Principle 5. The Father Wants You Actively to Seek and Trust His Protection

Look at what Scripture tells us we are to do regarding the Father's protection. It calls us to both attitudes and actions. (Underline the ways in which we are to actively seek and trust him.)

Trust in Him at all times, you people;
Pour out your heart before Him;
God is a refuge for us. (Ps. 62:8)

You will keep in perfect peace
him whose mind is steadfast,
because he trusts in you.
Trust in the LORD forever,
for the LORD, the LORD, is the Rock eternal.
(Isa. 26:3–4 NIV)

Let all who take refuge in you be glad;
let them ever sing for joy.
Spread your protection over them,
that those who love your name may rejoice in you.
For surely, O LORD, you bless the righteous;
you surround them with your favor as with a shield.
(Ps. 5:11–12 NIV)

If you make the Most High your dwelling—
even the LORD, who is my refuge—
then no harm will befall you,
no disaster will come near your tent.
For he will command his angels concerning you
to guard you in all your ways. . . .
"Because he loves me," says the LORD, "I will rescue him;
I will protect him, for he acknowledges my name.
He will call upon me, and I will answer him."
(Ps. 91:9–11, 14–15 NIV)

"O people of Zion, who live in Jerusalem, you will weep no more. How gracious he will be when you cry for help! As soon as he hears, he will answer you." (Isa. 30:19)

Did you note the words Scripture commands for us? When we face trouble, we are to pour out our hearts to him. Everybody trusts something; we must learn to trust the Lord, our eternal rock. We can take refuge in our Father God and make him our dwelling because he guards us. The Father wants us to actively seek his protection. When we are in danger, anxious, or afraid, he wants us to call on him, pour out our hearts to him, and run to him for help.

Author Ken Gire tells a story of a little girl who lived at the edge of a forest. One day she wandered off to explore all the dark secrets of the woods. The farther she wandered, the denser the woods became, until she totally lost her bearings and could not find her way back. As darkness descended, fear gripped her, and she screamed and sobbed until at last, in weariness, she fell asleep. Friends, family, and volunteers combed the area until the deep blackness of night thwarted their efforts. Early the next morning, as her father began his search afresh, he suddenly caught a glimpse of his little girl lying on a rock. Calling her by name, he ran as fast he could to her side. She was startled awake and threw her arms out to him. Wrapped in his tight embrace, she repeated over and over, "Daddy, I found you! Daddy, I found you!"

The little girl in this story sought and trusted her father's protection. She did everything she could to "find him." Even though in the end, it was the dad who found the girl and not the girl who found the dad, she took an active part in the process. In a similar manner, when we are distressed, our heavenly Father wants us actively to seek and trust him. He wants us to call and cry out for help. He wants us, for our diligence, to be able to exclaim, "Daddy, I found you!"

PRINCIPLE 6. THE FATHER WILL USE AFFLICTION FOR GOOD PURPOSES

A friend of mine once said, "I do not welcome pain, but I do not fear it. Pain is an excellent teacher." This thought is similar to what Grace said earlier in our journey. She said that the wisest, most godly people she knew were people who had walked through the deepest valleys. They were people familiar with pain.

Pain was not a part of life in the garden of Eden. Pain became a reality upon the entrance of sin into the world. Ultimately, the Father will do away with pain. At the end of time, when the dwelling of the Father is with his children, "He will wipe every tear from their eyes. There will be no more death or mourning or crying or pain" (Rev. 21:4 NIV).

Until such time, pain is a reality with which we all must wrestle. Because pain is an ever-present reality, the Father allows and uses it in the lives of his children for his own redemptive purposes. The following list represents some of the ways the Father will use pain in our lives:

- To bring correction to our behavior (Ps. 119:67)
- To teach us something about his character (Job 42:3–5)
- For testing and purification (Ps. 66:10)
- To bring us closer to his heart (Rom. 8:35–39)
- To increase our dependency upon him (2 Cor. 12:9)
- To increase our maturity and wisdom (James 1:2–5)
- To strengthen us (1 Pet. 5:10)
- To reveal his power and glory (John 9:1–3)

The Father desires to use the pain you encounter in your life to fulfill his purpose for you. That is one of the ways he protects you. He may not always protect you from pain, but he will protect you by redeeming the pain and changing it into something of eternal value. He uses what Satan meant for evil to build goodness in your life.

The choice to let the Father work in this way is yours. Contrast two passages of Scripture. Of those "who love God, to those who are the called according to His purpose," Romans 8:28 says, "in all things God works for the good" (NIV). On the other hand, in the parable of the soils Jesus told of "one who received the seed that fell on rocky places" (Matt. 13:20 NIV). That person received the word with joy, but when persecution came, Jesus said, "Since he has no root, he lasts only a short time. When trouble or persecution comes because of the word, he quickly falls away" (v. 21 NIV).

In the one case the person who loves God allows the Father to use pain and suffering for good purposes. In the other the persecution serves only to destroy the person's faith. In either case we see that the Father uses affliction. The question becomes, will affliction make you strong or simply prove you to be weak?

PRINCIPLE 7. THE FATHER PROVIDES A WAY OUT

The Father controls the boundaries around what can happen to us. First Corinthians 10:13 expands the principle with an additional bit of vital information. Regarding temptation, it says, "He makes the way of escape." Whatever situation we face, we need to learn to seek the Father's way out.

The theme of the book of 1 Peter is suffering. First Peter 5:10 tells us that "after you have suffered a little while, will himself restore you and make you strong, firm and steadfast" (NIV). Peter expected that the Father would allow the believers to suffer. The apostle recognized that the Father wanted to use suffering in their lives to make them strong, firm, and steadfast. I don't know about you, but I want those attributes.

Look with me at another passage of Scripture. This time we'll look to Psalm 34.

> The eyes of the LORD are on the righteous,
> And His ears are open to their cry. . . .
> The righteous cry out, and the LORD hears,
> And delivers them out of all their troubles.
> The LORD is near to those who have a broken heart,
> And saves such as have a contrite spirit.
> Many are the afflictions of the righteous,
> But the LORD delivers him out of them all.
> (Ps. 34:15, 17–19)

The Father sees and hears "the righteous." Who are the righteous? They are not those who are perfect and never do anything wrong. Rather the righteous are those who believe in Jesus and seek to live consistently as obedient children of God.

Did you see what the Father does when you cry out? He hears and delivers. The psalmist recognized that this truth does not mean a Pollyanna existence where nothing bad happens. Rather he saw a balance: "Many are the afflictions of the righteous, but the Lord delivers him out of them all."

Do you see the challenge in these verses? "Many afflictions" and "deliverance and salvation" go hand in hand. Christians are never guaranteed lives free from trouble. On the contrary, the Bible says that a righteous man may face *many* troubles. But it also teaches that at some point we will see the Father's deliverance. The Father delivers his children from every affliction. He may not deliver you when you want or in the way you want, but he *will* deliver you.

In Psalm 66, David said, "You let men ride over our heads; we went through fire and water, but you brought us to a place of abundance" (v. 12 NIV). The Father wants to use the pain and suffering you go through to bring you to a place of abundance. He does not enjoy seeing you suffer. He has promised that for every time of affliction, you can expect a time of deliverance and great victory.

That is why James encouraged Christians who had fallen into various trials to "count it all joy" (1:2). There is much joy in the protection of the Father, even in the midst of suffering. We do not rejoice in the pain of the trial but in the certainty of his protection, his deliverance and victory over the darkness.

In seeking the Father's protection, we actively seek his deliverance, and victory. We, like Paul, are wanting and expecting the God of peace to crush Satan under our feet (Rom. 16:20).

There are three mind-sets amongst believers regarding affliction. Some individuals resign themselves to the thought that God advocates suffering and, as a consequence, they do not look for his deliverance. Instead they wallow in self-pity, thinking that defeat and misery are hallmarks of spirituality. They are passive and fatalistic, crippled by the thought, *There's no way out.* On the opposite extreme, other believers think that suffering is unspiritual. They expect their lives to be characterized by a lack of hardship. When affliction comes, these individuals often take matters into their own hands and take their "own way out," which is generally the path of least resistance, the worldly response. They give up on a difficult marriage for example, rationalizing that God wants them to be happy and believing that divorce is the only road that will lead to happiness. Instead of looking for his way out, they take their own way out and spiritualize their decision to do so. The third way of responding is the only biblical one: It involves actively seeking the Father and following his lead, even if that means that more "men ride over our heads" or that we must walk through hotter "fire" and deeper "water." The biblical response is not passive, nor is it aggressive in forcing a quick resolution by taking matters into one's own hands. The biblical response involves active dependence. It involves waiting on God as well as doggedly pursuing his plan for victory and deliverance.

Let's review the seven principles of the Father's protection:
1. He sees.
2. He cares.

3. He will continually uphold you.
4. He will supply the strength you need.
5. He wants you actively to seek and trust him.
6. He will use affliction for good purposes.
7. He will provide a way out.

Are you currently going through a difficult trial in your life? If so, I urge you to pray all of the following:

- Acknowledge the Father's protection.
- Ask him to use the difficulty to bring good into your life.
- Ask him to help you see his way out and to deliver you.
- Ask him to help you keep your eyes on the certainty of his deliverance and victory.
- Thank him that ultimately he will crush Satan under your feet.

CHAPTER 16

FATHER GOD IS A
GENEROUS PROVIDER

My Father was not a great provider. It wasn't that he didn't work and earn money. It had more to do with his attitude. When Dad got his paycheck, he would go out and splurge, buying something expensive for himself: a better watch, a leather jacket, a better golf bag, or some new, wonderful gadget. Because of his splurging, we often would run out of money by the end of the month and were always in debt. He and Mom were always fighting about money. He grumbled and complained constantly about how much it cost to raise kids. There seemed to be enough money for him to go out with his friends but not enough for me to buy a present for my friend's birthday.

I know that my experience with my dad has affected my view of God the Father. I find it difficult to trust the Father to meet my needs. I do not like to depend on him. I prefer to be self-sufficient and self-reliant. I have this nagging suspicion that he, like my earthly dad, is going to let me down.

—Carmen

For everyone who asks receives, and he who seeks finds, and to him who knocks it will be opened. Or what man is there among you who, if his son asks for bread, will give him a stone? Or if he asks for a fish, will he give him a serpent? If you then, being evil, know how to give good gifts to your children, how much more will your Father who is in heaven give good things to those who ask Him! (Matt. 7:8–11)

"Then the Father will give you whatever you ask in my name."
(John 15:16 NIV)

"Ask, and you will receive, that your joy may be full."
(John 16:24)

"Again, I tell you that if two of you on earth agree about anything you ask for, it will be done for you by my Father in
heaven." (Matt. 18:19 NIV)

Government officials have made an increased effort in the past
few years to crack down on fathers who are delinquent in paying child
support. A father may not live with his child or even be involved in
her life, but society expects that biological fathers will, as a bare min-
imum, contribute financially to their child's well-being. Social service
agencies have little hope of forcing men to be good fathers, but at least
they can try to make them pay.

When a father is absent from the family unit, the financial income
of the family drops by an average of 60 to 70 percent. Therefore,
female-headed households make up the majority of families living
under the poverty line. This problem is called "the feminization of
poverty." Even women who receive child-support payments most
often struggle to make ends meet. When a father is present, the family
is far less likely to suffer. They are far less likely to be poor or in need.

David Blankenhorn, author of *Fatherless America* interviewed
hundreds of men who were married and living with their children. He
asked these men to describe what, in their minds, constituted a "good
father." All of the men interviewed said a good father provided for his
family.

This was not the only or even the most important characteristic
cited. However, in many cases, it was mentioned first. These men felt
that to be a good father they needed to be a good provider. Many of
them had wives who were employed outside of the home and who
contributed to the family income. Nevertheless they felt the father
bore the primary responsibility of provision. A good father willingly
and cheerfully works to provide for his family.

God the Father provides for his children. Provision is a primary
characteristic of his fatherhood. The Father is generous. He provides
for every need. He gives good gifts and a rich inheritance to each one
of his children.

A Generous Father

> Within the cluster of God's moral perfections there is one in particular to which the term goodness points. This is the quality of generosity. Generosity means a disposition to give to others in a way which has no mercenary motive and is not limited by what the recipients deserve, but consistently goes beyond it. Generosity expresses the simple wish that others should have what they need to make them happy. Generosity is, so to speak, the focal point of God's moral perfection; it is the quality which determines how all God's other excellences are to be displayed.
>
> —J. I. Packer[1]

God the Father has endless resources to meet the needs of his children. And he delights to use his resources for that purpose. He says, "I am God, your God! . . . Every beast of the forest is Mine, And the cattle on a thousand hills. I know all the birds of the mountains, And the wild beasts of the field are Mine. . . . For the world is Mine, and all its fullness. . . . Call upon Me; . . . I will deliver you" (Ps. 50:7, 10–12, 15).

In Psalm 81:10, the Father reassures his children that when they open their mouths wide he will fill them. This refers to a custom that existed during the time this psalm was written. When a benevolent king wished to extend a favor to a visitor or give an ambassador a special honor, he would request him to open his mouth wide. The king would then cram it full of sweetmeats. Occasionally he would even put in a handful of jewels. Consider the analogy of a generous monarch as you read these words from Scripture:

> I will bless her with abundant provisions; her poor will I satisfy with food. (Ps. 132:15 NIV)

> You gave abundant showers, O God; you refreshed your weary inheritance. Your people settled in it, and from your bounty, O God, you provided for the poor. (Ps. 68:9–10 NIV)

The children of Israel often questioned the ability of the Father to provide. They asked, "Can God spread a table in the desert? When he struck the rock, water gushed out, and streams flowed abundantly. But can he also give us food? Can he supply meat for his people?" (Ps. 78:19–20 NIV).

The Father had provided for his children supernaturally. He had opened the doors of heaven and rained down manna; "Men ate angels' food" (v. 25). The Father had sent them "food to the full" (v. 25). Yet the psalmist laments, in spite of his wonderful provision, they did not trust in his provision (v. 32).

The children of Israel did not see that the things they had were given by the Father's hand. They did not acknowledge that it was he who gave the grain, the new wine and oil, and lavished silver and gold on them (Hos. 2:8). When they had plenty, they did not recognize that it was he who had given it. And when it looked as though they might be in need, they complained, turned away, and blamed God for not providing. Their problem was not that the Father failed to provide. It was that they failed to see and recognize his generosity.

THE FATHER PROVIDES FOR OUR NEEDS

Jesus talked extensively about the provision of the Father. He said that the example of the birds and wildflowers show that the Father is aware of all of our physical needs:

> Don't fuss about what's on the table at mealtimes or whether the clothes in your closet are in fashion. There is far more to your life than the food you put in your stomach, more to your outer appearance than the clothes you hang on your body. Look at the birds, free and unfettered, not tied down to a job description, careless in the care of God. And you count far more to him than birds. . . .

> If God gives such attention to the appearance of wildflowers— most of which are never even seen—don't you think he'll attend to you, take pride in you, do his best for you? What I'm trying to do here is to get you to relax, to not be so preoc- cupied with *getting*, so you can respond to God's *giving*. People who don't know God and the way he works fuss over these things, but you know both God and how he works. Steep your life in God-reality, God-initiative, God-provisions. Don't worry

about missing out. You'll find all your everyday human concerns will be met. (Matt. 6:25–26, 30–33 *The Message*)

I love the way Eugene Peterson described depending on God's provision. Are you "careless" in the care of the Father? Wouldn't you like to be?

Said the robin to the sparrow, "I should really like to know
why do these anxious human beings rush about and worry
so."
Said the sparrow to the robin, "I think it must be
they have no heavenly Father such as cares for you and me."

Think about this old poem for a moment. If these birds were watching you, do you think they would see anxiety and worry in your life, or would they observe you trusting the Father? Do you trust in the care and provision of your heavenly Father? Why do you think you feel the way you do? And, possibly the most important question, how can you become more like a sparrow?

THE FATHER GIVES GOOD GIFTS

Jesus used the example of earthly fathers to argue for the generosity of the heavenly Father. He reasoned that if earthly fathers, who are inherently evil, know how to give good gifts to their kids, how much more would the heavenly Father, who is perfect, know how to do so?

For everyone who asks receives; he who seeks finds; and to him who knocks, the door will be opened. Which of you, if his son asks for bread, will give him a stone? Or if he asks for a fish, will give him a snake? If you, then, though you are evil, know how to give good gifts to your children, how much more will your Father in heaven give good gifts to those who ask him! (Matt. 7:8–11 NIV)

James said that every good gift and every perfect gift are from above and come down from the Father (1:17). Think of some of the good gifts the Father gives you. Psalm 112:9 says that

God "has scattered abroad his gifts" (NIV). Has the Father "scattered" gifts toward you?

THE FATHER HAS AN INHERITANCE FOR HIS CHILDREN

I was speaking with my parents a few months ago, and they mentioned that they had just reviewed their life insurance plan and will. They said they wanted to make sure that everything was in order so that we children would be sure to receive an inheritance. I got off the phone and sighed. My parents are well into their retirement years, and it may not be long until they die. No inheritance in the world could take their place. I would much rather have them than any inheritance they could leave me.

When God the Father adopted us as his children, he qualified us to share in the family inheritance (Col. 1:12). His inheritance is rich and glorious (Eph. 1:18). It can never perish, spoil, or fade (1 Pet. 1:4). The Father is keeping it in heaven for us as a reward for our faith and patience (1 Pet. 1:4; Heb. 6:12; Col. 3:24). In the meantime he has given us the Holy Spirit as a "deposit" (Eph. 1:11–14 NIV).

Paul tells us that our inheritance is the kingdom of Christ and the Father (Eph. 5:5). The difference between my earthly father's and my heavenly Father's inheritance strikes me as most ironic. For the former I will be separated from the father I love in order to receive an inheritance of things I can't keep forever. For the latter I will leave the things I can't keep in order forever to be together with the Father I love.

If you could have only one inheritance, which would you honestly choose? Would you rather have an inheritance of money and earthly riches or an eternal relationship with the Father?

Good fathers work hard to try to ensure that their children are blessed with an inheritance. As providers, they are concerned with providing for more than the moment. They try to provide for the future so their children will be secure. Father God has provided for our future. He has guaranteed that all of his children will be blessed with a glorious, eternal inheritance that can never perish, spoil, or fade.

The Father Wants Us to Ask

So many of us live like spiritual paupers rather than children of the King. Why is this so? James, the brother of Jesus, taught that the reason we do not have is that we do not ask or that we ask with the wrong motives (James 4:2–3). Jesus taught his disciples to ask the Father for their daily needs: "Give us this day our daily bread" (Matt. 6:11). But why should we ask the Father for things when he already knows our needs? The simplest answer to this question is that the Father likes to be asked. "We like our children to ask us for things that we already know they need because the very asking enhances and deepens the relationship. . . . Love loves to be told what it knows already. It wants to be asked for what it longs to give."[2]

The Father wants us to ask so that our desire for the gift leads and directs us toward a desire for the giver. God is not an absentee Father who impersonally sends child support. His provision is deeply personal and is grounded in intimacy of relationship with his children.

The Father is a good provider. He longs to provide for our every need. He has already provided an astounding inheritance for our future. What he requires of us, in order to pour out the bounty of his provision, is merely that we continually seek his face and ask.

Conclude this chapter by talking to the Father. Acknowledge that the Father is a generous provider and that he longs to have you approach him with your needs. Take a moment right now to ask him for whatever needs you have.

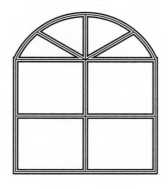

PART 4

Getting to Know God as Father: Father God Is Devoted to You

"The LORD your God is with you,
he is mighty to save.
He will take great delight in you,
he will quiet you with his love,
he will rejoice over you with singing."

—ZEPHANIAH 3:17 NIV

If God represents Himself as a father, perhaps it is because He knows best what a father's love should represent. The offense is born in the heart of someone who has failed to understand that a father is a compliment to a woman and not an insult. Sadly, we have come to a time when the role of the father has been so mutilated that we have lost any real revelation into the breadth and depth of the Father's heart. How could any daughter be offended who has ever seen the broadening grin on the leathery face of a compassionate father whose greatest joy is seeing his daughter succeed?

A good father is not an insult to femininity. A good father is an avid fan of his daughter, a source of insulation from insult and adversity. He is there for her. He nurtures her.

—T. D. Jakes[1]

CHAPTER 17

THE FATHER DELIGHTS IN YOU

My husband, Dave, changed dramatically after our first child, Amanda, was born. I think it was the responsibility of being a good father that motivated the change. He stopped swearing, stopped drinking, stopped staying out late, and started to go to church. He began to look past himself and pour himself out for her.

I have never seen Dave so happy. He absolutely delights in Amanda. He can hardly wait to get home from work to cuddle her, take her for a piggyback ride, play ball, or sit on the floor and play with the Fisher Price farm. It is amazing to hear this grown man clucking and mooing and braying with such inhibition. He is totally enraptured with his little girl. The feeling is mutual. All afternoon she asks, "When Daddy be home?" When she hears his car in the driveway, she bolts to the door, squealing with delight. The joy of their daily five o'clock reunion resembles that of passionate lovers that have been apart for months instead of just hours.

I did not have a great relationship with my father. And I haven't really developed much of a relationship with my heavenly Father. But watching Dave with our little girl helps me understand more about the fatherhood of God. Dave is enraptured. He is totally abandoned with joy and a deep heart commitment to his girl. It has made me think and hope that the heavenly Father's heart might just be the same way toward me.

—Darlene

The Lord your God is with you,
　　he is mighty to save.
He will take great delight in you,

he will quiet you with his love,
he will rejoice over you with singing. (Zeph. 3:17 NIV)

What then shall we say to these things? If God is for us, who
can be against us? (Rom. 8:31)

In the next chapters of our journey, we will study the devotion of
the Father. You will see that he is totally devoted to you. Because
of this, he is dependable; he guides, corrects, and is patient and forgiving. But most of all you will see that the Father is 100 percent
behind you. He will never forget you or desert you. He delights in you.
He is your biggest and most loyal fan.

YOU ARE THE DELIGHT OF HIS HEART

In recent years as I have considered the aspects of God's fatherhood, Zephaniah 3:17 has become an absolute favorite verse for me. It
tells me that God is mighty to save, but it gets far more specific than
that. It says that God does three wonderful things for me. These three
actions reveal his love for me in a way that touches the deep places of
my soul.

The LORD your God is with you, he is mighty to save. He will
take great delight in you, he will quiet you with his love, he
will rejoice over you with singing. (Zeph. 3:17 NIV)

What a beautiful picture of the Father heart of God! When I read
this verse, I imagine a father holding his young daughter in the middle of the night, rocking her and soothing her back to sleep with
gentle, tender songs of love. The lessons reflected in this verse are
profound.

- The Father is with you no matter how dark the night or how
  difficult the problem.
- He is mighty—your strong Father with whom you can feel safe
  and secure.
- He will save you, protecting and delivering you from the evil
  one.
- He delights in you; you are the pride and joy of his heart.
- He quiets you, soothing your fears and giving you confidence
  and peace.

- He rejoices over you with singing, with sweet songs of tender love.

Have you ever considered that you are the delight of the Father's heart? You are his special girl. Or, if you happen to be a male reading this volume, you get to be his special boy. He sees you as the one who can bring him great joy. The one in whom he takes great pleasure. The one of whom he is proud. The one with whom he is enraptured.

Can you imagine the Father rejoicing over you with singing? He does, you know, whenever your heart is inclined toward him.

Imagine this. The Scripture tells us that delight is how the Father feels about his son, Jesus. The Father called Jesus "my chosen one in whom I delight" (Isa. 42:1 NIV). At Jesus' baptism the Father's voice thundered with pride from heaven, saying, "This is my Son, whom I love; with him I am well pleased" (Matt. 3:17 NIV).

Delight was in God's heart when he created mankind (Prov. 8:30–31). He delighted in Abraham, Isaac, and Jacob (Deut. 10:15), and in David (2 Sam. 22:20). But he did not delight in Saul's outward appearance of religiosity (1 Sam. 15:22). Nor does he delight in those who do evil (Mal. 2:17). The Father delights in all those whose hearts are inclined toward him to obey his word.

The following list represents some of the attitudes that the Father delights in. As you read each one, consider whether you honestly try to have that particular attitude in your life. He delights in those who:

- Seek to obey his voice (1 Sam. 15:22)
- Have a teachable spirit (Prov. 3:12)
- Have a broken and contrite heart (Ps. 51:16–17)
- Try to walk blamelessly (Prov. 11:20)
- Deal truthfully (Prov. 12:22)
- Pray with an upright heart (Prov. 15:8)
- Demonstrate mercy (Mic. 7:18)
- Demonstrate kindness, justice, and righteousness (Jer. 9:24)

The Father delights in all those children who are living as members of his family. Have you accepted the fact that the Father delights in you? And are you comfortable with the idea of the Father delighting in you?

Beware of letting the legalistic lie that you can please God with your good works cloud the issue. The Father delights in his children. His delight has nothing to do with any virtue or greatness in the child but only because of his great love and faithfulness. He is the ultimate good Father.

HE IS YOUR BIGGEST FAN

One year my son Matthew was on an ice hockey team called the Green Gators. While some of the fathers were coaching the boys in hockey skills, one particularly enthusiastic mom was coaching the remaining parents in how to be good fans. She organized us into one of the most boisterous cheering squads minor hockey has ever seen.

We waved green and gold pompoms. We stamped our feet. We chanted, did the wave and our Gator Snap. More than once during a game, the eyes of the players from both teams, as well as all the coaches and referees, were directed with fascination toward the stands, where middle-aged women dressed in baggy sweatshirts were exuberantly doing the macarena. (I hope there is no video footage to commemorate the event!)

Although I took part in cheering for the Gators team, the real reason I was there was Matthew. It was he whom my eyes followed as he skated around the ice. It was he who really thrilled my heart when he scored. And my heart froze, gripped with fear, when the body that went into the boards and lay motionless on the ice was his.

If it weren't for Matthew, I wouldn't have been at all those games. If it weren't for him, I would not have cared about the Gators. (And I certainly wouldn't have been doing the macarena!)

I am Matthew's number one fan. I am also Clark's and Jonathan's number one fan. They may not ever make the NHL or even be very good players, but they are the absolute best in my eyes. Of course they are! They are my children. And my heart belongs to them forever in a way that it does not belong to anyone else.

The Father is your number one fan. His eyes are continually on you. He is thrilled when you play the best you can. And when you manage to score a goal, he and the throngs of angels in heaven cheer. Who knows, they may even do the macarena. (Probably not, but it could happen!)

His heart is gripped when you fall. He is right there for you. He will pick you up and rub down all of your bruised, sore muscles. He will encourage you and coach you and help you get back in the game.

The heart of the Father belongs to His children in a way that it does not belong to anyone else. Malachi 3:17 tells us that his children are his most cherished treasure.

In fact, Scripture is full of verses that describe you as treasure to the Father. Isaiah predicted that, "You will be a crown of splendor in the LORD's hand, a royal diadem in the hand of your God" (Isa. 62:3 NIV). Zechariah said of God's children, "They will sparkle in his land like jewels in a crown. How attractive and beautiful they will be!" (Zech. 9:16–17 NIV).

"Crown of splendor," "royal diadem," and "jewels in a crown" all refer to the most significant piece of jewelry owned by a ruling monarch. The crown is said to be priceless. It is the most treasured possession of the king. He alone has the right to wear it.

After proclaiming that his children are his treasure, God continues, "You will be called Hephzibah [means "my delight is in her"] . . . for the LORD will take delight in you . . . as a bridegroom rejoices over his bride, so will your God rejoice over you" (Isa. 62:4–5 NIV).

The Father is undeniably for you. He delights in you. You are his treasure. He rejoices over you. He is totally committed to your happiness and well-being. And if God is for you, who can be against you? (Rom. 8:31).

Rayna said of her earthly father: "He was always my biggest fan. I knew he believed in me and would always be there for me. This knowledge gave me the confidence to stretch my wings and fly higher than I ever could have without his support."

Do you know and believe that your heavenly Father is truly for you? Does this knowledge increase your confidence? Close this chapter by asking the Father to help you feel his pleasure shining on you. Thank him that he delights in you and is totally devoted to you. Ask him for increased confidence to spread your wings and fly higher, buoyed by his strength and support.

CHAPTER 18

THE FATHER IS DEPENDABLE

My Father was unpredictable. A glass of spilled milk could be met with laughter and joking, or it could be met with the full fury of his anger and a beating. I was never sure how he would react or what he would do. The whole atmosphere of the house seemed to change when he walked through the door. All play or conversation would pause as we tried to read his mood. I felt insecure and timid in his presence. I wanted to please him and gain his approval but was not certain how to do it.

My experience with my father has deeply affected my perception of myself and of God the Father. I am afraid of people. I strive to please them and hope that I can do the right things to make them like me. I am also timid about approaching God the Father. I feel that if I tiptoe around and avoid doing anything drastically wrong, I might be able to keep him happy. I'm not sure though. I suspect that he might get angry with me anyhow.

—Dori

For no matter how many promises God has made, they are "Yes" in Christ. And so through him the "Amen" is spoken by us to the glory of God. (2 Cor. 1:20 NIV)

Yet the LORD longs to be gracious to you;
he rises to show you compassion.
For the LORD is a God of justice.
Blessed are all who wait for him! (Isa. 30:18 NIV)

One day at the playground, Brent and I were standing beneath the slide chatting while our firstborn son, Clark, then a preschooler, was clambering up.

"Catch me, Daddy!" Clark shouted, as he jumped from the full height down toward Brent. Brent turned to see Clark already sailing through the air and just managed to do a football-type lunge to catch him. Clark had jumped at the same time he had called. He didn't wait to ask Brent to catch him. He just assumed that he would. "Daddy always catches me!"

Clark is now a young man. For the past few weeks he has been asking Brent and me to buy a supercharged, high-speed computer. He approaches us when we are preoccupied with other things—in the middle of a conversation, working on the computer, or even when we are on the phone. He slips a picture or description of his dream computer under our noses and whispers, "Can we get it?"

I was really getting annoyed. I asked Clark why he was bothering us in this way instead of waiting for an appropriate moment to talk. He smiled and said, "I was hoping to catch you in a moment of weakness, to get you to say yes just to get me to stop bothering you. Once you say yes, you'll have to do it. You're always true to your word."

These stories illustrate the trust of a child in the faithfulness of his parents. When he was young, Clark trusted his dad to catch him because he knew his dad was big enough to do so and because his dad had always caught him in the past. Now that he is older, Clark trusts his dad and me to be true to our word. So much so, that he attempts to coerce us into giving our word because he is confident that we cannot and will not fail to fulfill it.

To be *faithful* means "to be unswervingly devoted; loyal to one's promises; trustworthy; sure, firm, certain." It means predictability in a good, wholesome, positive sense. Those who are trustworthy are consistent in character with regard to their loyalty toward you. They are also true to what they say they will do. They will not disappoint you or let you down. You can totally trust and depend on them.

Whom do you consider to be the most faithful person in your life? Your father? Mother? A friend? Your husband? No one? What about God? Do you feel that God the Father is faithful to you?

FAITHFUL FATHER

We all long to have someone in our lives on whom we can count. If your father or another significant figure in you life has been unfaithful to you, you may struggle with fear of rejection, hurt, humiliation, anxiety, and/or feelings of inferiority. Faithlessness breeds emotional insecurities in one's life. Faithfulness, on the other hand, fosters security, confidence, permission to fail, and the ability to be vulnerable to others.

Faithfulness is one of the Father's prime characteristics. He revealed himself to Moses as "the faithful God" who keeps his promise of love (Deut 7:9). Paul often reminded the early believers of this trait. "God is faithful, by whom you were called into the fellowship of His Son" (1 Cor. 1:9). "The one who calls you is faithful and he will do it" (1 Thess. 5:24 NIV).

The Father has "no variation or shadow due to change" (James 1:17 RSV). He remains totally consistent in character (Ps. 102:25–27). He is not, like Dori's father, one way today and a different way tomorrow. His faithfulness is not affected by mood swings or circumstances. His faithfulness is "perfect" (Isa. 25:1 NIV), established in heaven itself (Ps. 89:2). The Father is faithful without flaw. And he remains faithful forever (Ps. 146:6).

The Father is faithful because he loves you. He would never let you down. It would go against his nature. In fact, according to Paul, it is impossible for the Father to let you down. To him, not being faithful is as remote a possibility as not loving or not being God. The Father is faithful. He is faithful because he is God: "If we are faithless, He remains faithful; He cannot deny Himself" (2 Tim. 2:13). According to 2 Timothy 2:13, it is possible for humans to be undependable, inconsistent, and untrustworthy. It is impossible for the Father to be any of those things.

Second Corinthians 1:20 says, "No matter how many promises God has made, they are 'Yes' in Christ. And so through him the 'Amen' is spoken by us to the glory of God." *Amen* means "certainly, always, truly, for sure"! I can be sure, without a doubt, that the Father will do what he says.

A few months ago I bought a fitness club membership for one of my sons. My husband and I made the decision based on that particular son's needs. When my youngest son found out, he protested with cries of "No fair!" He felt as though we had done him a great injustice. But his perception of justice is different from ours. We are the parents. He is the child. We make decisions taking into account factors he has no awareness of. As parents, we continually make decisions that our children could perceive as unfair. We paid for braces for one son's teeth. But not all of our sons got braces. We bought a new pair of Rollerblades for one son; the other got secondhand ones. One son gets guitar lessons; the other goes to drama. One is required to paint the fence; the other does data entry at the office.

We love our children equally, but we interact with them differently based on their age, their personality, their gifts, the character traits they need to develop in their lives, and a myriad of other factors, some of which have nothing to do with them at all. Our love and their equality of worth do not demand that we treat them exactly the same. According to my children, this sometimes appears unfair. But we know better. We are more mature and have a better sense of justice than they.

Justice means acting in accordance with what is right. It signifies "straightness" or acting correctly. The Father is just. He acts correctly. "He is the Rock, his works are perfect, and all his ways are just. A faithful God who does no wrong, upright and just is he" (Deut. 32:4 NIV).

Psalm 97:2 declares that righteousness and justice are the foundation of his throne. Psalm 45:6 says, "Your throne, O God, will last for ever and ever; a scepter of justice will be the scepter of your kingdom" (NIV). Those passages tell me that justice is no passing whim for our God. Justice is so built into the fabric of his nature that from eternity past to eternity future he will never for one moment act in any way that is not just.

Many people suffer the earthly tragedy of parental injustice. When such injustice arises, whether in your past or present, you can do at least two things. You can draw the mistaken conclusion that God is also unfair, or you can learn to see earthly injustice as a contrast to God's character. Just as the black night is necessary to appreciate the brilliance of a sunrise, earthly injustice is but the absence of God's justice, and Scripture tells us that such injustice is but a precursor of the glory that is to follow.

The psalmist described justice as the foundation of the throne of God and the scepter of his kingdom. A foundation is the base on which a structure rests. A scepter is a mark of royal authority. The verses above teach that the justice of God is the characteristic on which the rule of God stands. He rules as King because he is correct and without error.

Have you ever thought that the Father was unfair? Have you wondered why he does not punish those who harm you? Why others are more talented or beautiful or athletic than you? Or why they appear to have more and better spiritual gifts? Do you question why he heals one person and not another? Or why he has appointed your husband and not you to be the head of your home? Have you ever cried out: "Father, it's not fair!"? I have.

I do not know the answers to the questions. I do not know why. But I do know that just as my sense of justice is more perfect than my children's, so the Father's sense of justice is more perfect than mine. Human justice is so inferior to the Father's justice that Solomon could say, "There is not a just man on earth" (Eccl. 7:20).

David said that the Father's righteousness is like the mighty mountains and his justice like the great deep (Ps. 36:6). This is a fitting analogy, for the ways of the Father are too high and too deep for us to comprehend fully. We cannot always know why, but we do know that the Father is just, good, kind, loving, and faithful.

Proclaim "Yes!" and "Amen!" to some promises of the Father. Here is my suggested prayer:

Dear Father, I proclaim your faithfulness. When all others disappoint me and let me down, you will be faithful to me. You have loved me with an everlasting love (Jer. 31:3). You have plans for my well-being. Your plans give me hope and a secure future (Jer. 29:11). Your ways are good and right and fair. I am blessed as I wait for you to fulfill your promises (Isa. 30:18). I can hold unswervingly to the hope I profess in you. You have promised! You will not let me down! You are faithful (Heb. 10:23). I proclaim these things, for they are true, Father. I proclaim the truth for your glory in Jesus' name. Amen.

CHAPTER 19

THE FATHER GUIDES

I really miss my dad. He died two years ago. The thing I miss most is being able to call him and ask advice. Dad always gave great advice! It was thoughtful, wise, challenging, sometimes rebuking or correcting, but always loving and gentle. I could take all of my life's crazy messes and disappointments to him. His advice would never fail to provide perspective, clarity, and hope.

When I think of my heavenly Father, I imagine him to be like my dad. I imagine myself grabbing a Coke, plunking down on the sofa across from the easy chair where he sits and saying, "Dad, I need some advice." I find myself doing that a lot now. I can't always hear God as clearly as I heard my dad, but I know that if my dad's advice and guidance were so valuable, then my heavenly Dad's will be even better.

—Michelle

The Lord will guide you continually,
and satisfy your soul in drought,
And strengthen your bones;
You shall be like a watered garden,
And like a spring of water, whose waters do not fail.
(Isa. 58:11)

I will lead the blind by ways they have not known,
along unfamiliar paths I will guide them;
I will turn the darkness into light before them
and make the rough places smooth.
These are the things I will do;
I will not forsake them. (Isa. 42:16)

They will feed beside the roads
and find pasture on every barren hill.
They will neither hunger nor thirst,
nor will the desert heat or the sun beat upon them.
He who has compassion on them will guide them
and lead them beside springs of water.
I will turn all my mountains into roads,
and my highways will be raised up. (Isa. 49:9–11 NIV)

Show me your ways, O LORD,
teach me your paths;
guide me in your truth and teach me,
for you are God my Savior,
and my hope is in you all day long. (Ps. 25:4–5 NIV)

Fathers play an important role in guiding their children. A responsible father seeks to train his children to live right. He provides encouragement and enables them to find meaning, purpose, and direction for their lives. He fosters his children's talents, education, and career choices. He also teaches his children many practical skills. Guiding and training one's children is a duty that responsible fathers take seriously.

I asked my friend Robert to reflect on the nature of his "father heart" for his daughter. This is what he said:

Let me try articulating the nature of my father-daughter relationship this way: I am preparing her to be a bride, but I am not the groom. I am preparing her to be a mother, but I am neither the husband nor the child. I am preparing her to be a godly woman, but I am not female. How am I preparing her? By being a man of integrity and love in her life, I am trying to be the proto-man against which she can evaluate the character of men to come. How is this preparation different for the boys? Well, the focus is different: the boys are to be godly men, husbands, and fathers, which I exerted to role model for them. And the position is different—that is to say, I prepare my sons from the position of being a man; I do not prepare my daughter to be a woman from the position of being a woman.

I found Robert's reply fascinating. I had asked him to reflect on his father heart of love for his daughter. I had expected that he would express something about his emotions or feelings. But instead his focus was on his responsibility and commitment to train, guide, and prepare her for the future. Training his daughter to be a godly woman is at the center of his father heart of love for her.

A good father trains and guides his children to a place of maturity and wholeness. A good father helps his children grow up into responsible adulthood. A good father is not content that his children remain at the level they are. He challenges them to reach for what can be. He always has an eye toward the future.

King Solomon described his responsibility to his children:

> Listen, my sons, to a father's instruction;
> pay attention and gain understanding.
> I give you sound learning,
> so do not forsake my teaching.
> When I was a boy in my father's house,
> still tender, and an only child of my mother,
> he taught me and said,
> "Lay hold of my words with all your heart;
> keep my commands and you will live.
> Get wisdom, get understanding;
> do not forget my words or swerve from them."
> . . . Listen, my son, accept what I say,
> and the years of your life will be many.
> I guide you in the way of wisdom
> and lead you along straight paths.
> When you walk, your steps will not be hampered;
> when you run, you will not stumble.
> Hold on to instruction, do not let it go;
> guard it well, for it is your life. . . .
> My son, pay attention to what I say;
> listen closely to my words.
> Do not let them out of your sight,
> keep them within you heart;
> for they are life to those who find them.
> (Prov. 4:1–5, 10–13, 20–22 NIV)

King Solomon guided his children in the way of wisdom. He urged them to listen to his advice. Obviously, following the advice of our earthly father is not always wise. Our earthly fathers' advice is fallible because all humans are sinners. But our heavenly Father does not share human defects or weaknesses.

Your earthly father does not always have the character, the wisdom, or the right information to give you the best advice. But your heavenly Father does. God is the perfect Father. And as a perfect Father, he teaches and guides his children perfectly.

God said of the children of Israel, "I trained them and strengthened them" (Hos. 7:15 NIV). Isaiah prophesied, "All your children shall be taught by the LORD, And great shall be the peace of your children" (Isa. 54:13). Jesus may have been referring to this verse when he said, "Everyone who listens to the Father and learns from him comes to me" (John 6:45 NIV).

God the Father wants you to be at ease asking him for guidance. He knows what is best. He does not have any personal quirks, biases, or misinformation that would cause him to guide you contrary to your best interest. He loves you perfectly. He has perfect awareness of your situation. He has perfect wisdom. Therefore, seeking his advice is not only advisable; it is absolutely essential to your well-being.

The Father expects that his children will turn to him for guidance. When the children of Israel failed to do so, He lamented, "How gladly would I treat you like sons. . . . I thought you would call me 'Father' and not turn away from following me" (Jer. 3:19 NIV). The Father guides from a heart of love, and his children are expected to follow obediently.

King David said, "Direct me in the path of your commands, for there I find delight" (Ps. 119:35). Do you delight in the way of the Father? Do you enjoy seeking and listening to his advice? Can you imagine yourself grabbing a Coke, plunking down on the sofa across from the easy chair where he sits and saying, "Dad, I need some advice"?

Psalm 25:4–5 gives us a wonderful model prayer asking for God's guidance:

> Show me your ways, O LORD,
> teach me your paths;
> guide me in your truth and teach me,
> for you are God my Savior,
> and my hope is in you all day long. (NIV)

CHAPTER 20

THE FATHER CORRECTS US

My dad was great fun. My childhood memories are mostly of laughter and play. Dad could make a game out of anything. In a sense he was my best friend. But he was more than a friend. He was my father. Therefore, unlike a friend, he had clear expectations for my behavior. I experienced his discipline when I rebelled or neglected the boundaries. Although we often laughed and played together, I needed to respect and obey him.

I remember one occasion when I stole a chocolate bar from the store. I confessed when Dad confronted me about the sticky foil wrapper that had fallen out of my pocket. I'll never forget the look of disappointment on his face. With eyes filled with tears, he said, "And now, Anya, you know what I must do."

I did know. He had to discipline me. He took me by the hand, and we walked back to the store. After I apologized to the owner, Dad and he decided that I would wash shelves as discipline. It took me two days to wash all of the shelves. Each day Dad walked me to the store after school and came to pick me up before supper.

I learned a good lesson from that experience and from all the other times when my dad disciplined me. I knew that his correction was a part of his love. He could not allow me to get away with doing wrong, for that would harm me, and he did not want me to be harmed. The correction, though sometimes painful in and of itself, actually saved me from pain in the long run.

—Anya

My son, do not despise the chastening of the LORD,
Nor detest His correction;
For whom the LORD loves He corrects,
Just as a father the son in whom he delights.
(Prov. 3:11–12)

He who instructs the nations, shall He not correct,
He who teaches man knowledge? (Ps. 94:10)

"Behold, happy is the man whom God corrects;
Therefore do not despise the chastening of the Almighty.
For He bruises, but He binds up;
He wounds, but His hands make whole." (Job 5:17–18)

"He who ignores discipline despises himself. . . . The fear of
the Lord teaches a man wisdom, and humility comes before
honor." (Prov. 15:32–33 NIV)

Beth and Susan were playing. Both had been warned by their
fathers to stay out of the construction-area mud in the back lane, but
it had proved to be irresistible. Making and tossing mud pies was just
too much fun. By the time they had finished playing, they had mud on
their clothing, mud all over their boots, mud on the fence, and a
muddy track of footprints all the way down the sidewalk.

As time for supper neared, they began to realize that they would
soon be facing their fathers. Beth was heartbroken and ashamed. She
realized she would have to confess, ask for forgiveness, and face the
consequences of her behavior. She figured that her father would make
her stay home from girl's club that evening in order to clean the mess
she had made. She slowly began to walk toward her house with her
head hanging low.

Susan was terrified. She began to tremble. The thought of facing
her father and confessing was more than she could bear. She knew he
would scream and swear at her. And, if he had had a hard day, the beating would be especially severe. Furthermore, after being humiliated,
she could expect to be forbidden to play with Beth for at least a week.
Susan began to devise a plan to deceive her father. Perhaps she could
sneak home and change her clothes without him noticing. She would
try to hide her disobedience and avoid him for as long as possible. She

would lie if necessary. Susan crept home through the bushes, pausing to hide her muddy boots under the juniper.

All children receive correction. For most of us, our father played a significant role in correcting our childhood behavior. Some of us will relate to Beth. Our father corrected our behavior with love, consistency, and justice. We regarded his discipline as good, albeit painful. Others of us relate to Susan. Our father may have been harsh or even abusive in his attempts to bring correction into our lives. Because of our experience, we may resent and even hate the thought of discipline.

Do you relate to any of the following statements?

- My father did not correct me. He was not at all involved in my life.
- My father was permissive. He rarely disciplined me for wrong behavior.
- My father was inconsistent. I never knew when I would be disciplined or what type of discipline to expect.
- My father was loving, fair, and consistent in his correction.
- My father was harsh and overly punitive. The discipline was often more severe than the offense warranted.
- My father was abusive. He berated and/or beat me for little or no reason.

Correcting one's children is one of the tasks of responsible fatherhood. God corrects us because he is our Father. But, contrary to the faulty examples of correction that we often see in earthly fathers, our heavenly Father's correction is always loving, fair, and consistent. It is also tempered by his great mercy.

THE FATHER CORRECTS BECAUSE HE LOVES

Correction, when properly administered, is an expression of love. King Solomon, the wisest man who ever lived, said that fathers who love their children are careful to correct them. Furthermore, fathers who withhold discipline are doing their children a great disservice. So great is this disservice, Solomon argued, that in essence, through lack of correction, these fathers demonstrate that they do not love but in actual fact hate their children (Prov. 13:24 NIV).

Proverbs 3:11–12 shows the Father's attitude toward those whom he rebukes, disciplines, and corrects: "My son, do not despise the

LORD's discipline and do not resent his rebuke, because the LORD disciplines those he loves, as a father the son he delights in" (NIV).

To *chasten* means "to inflict suffering upon for the purpose of moral improvement; to discipline and mold character through adversity." Chastening differs from punishment in that it is redemptive. Its purpose is not vengeance or humiliation. It is motivated by love and commitment to the person's best interests.

THE FATHER'S CORRECTION IS FOR YOUR BENEFIT

Psalm 94:10 says, "Does he who disciplines nations not punish? Does he who teaches man lack knowledge?" (NIV). The Father's correction is always associated with teaching. Correction is the other side of guidance. It is simply another way we are trained or instructed. Parents who are permissive don't help their children mature. On the contrary, their permissiveness and lack of correction often turn their children into monsters.

Our Father doesn't want his children to be spoiled monsters. He corrects us as part of guiding us to maturity. Correction is part of our education. It is part of him loving us.

The following paraphrase of Hebrews 12:5–11 comes from *The Message*. Notice how many times Eugene Peterson used the words *training* and *educating*. Look for the phrases that indicate the Father's correction is an expression of his love:

So don't feel sorry for yourselves. Or have you forgotten how good parents treat children, and that God regards you as his children?

My dear child, don't shrug off God's discipline,
but don't be crushed by it either.
It's the child he loves that he disciplines;
the child he embraces, he also corrects.

God is educating you; that's why you must never drop out. He's treating you as dear children. This trouble you're in isn't punishment; it's training, the normal experience of children. Only irresponsible parents leave children to fend for themselves. Would you prefer an irresponsible God? We respect our own parents for training and not spoiling us, so why not embrace God's training so we can truly live? While we were children, our parents did what seemed best to them. But God is doing what is best for us, training us to live God's holy best. At the time, discipline isn't much fun. It always feels like it's going against the grain. Later, of course, it pays off handsomely, for it's the well-trained who find themselves mature in their relationship with God.

The purpose of fatherly correction is training. In Ephesians 6:4, Paul instructs fathers that they ought not "exasperate" their children with discipline but to correct in such a way that the child will accept the training and instruction of the Lord. He repeats the same sort of instruction to the fathers in Colosse: "Fathers, do not embitter your children, or they will become discouraged" (Col. 3:21 NIV).

Discipline that is harsh, unjustified, or wrongly motivated can exasperate, embitter, and discourage. But the correction of the Father, though difficult, is always gentle. He always corrects for your benefit. He desires to bring you to a place of deeper maturity, wisdom, and joy.

Job said, "Blessed is the man whom God corrects; so do not despise the discipline of the Almighty. For he wounds, but he also binds up; he injures, but his hands also heal" (Job 5:17–18 NIV).

Scripture outlines many ways God corrects:
- Through his Word (2 Tim. 3:16)
- Through his Holy Spirit convicting of sin (John 16:7–8)
- Through visions and prophecy (Acts 10:9–16; 2 Sam. 12:1–15)
- Through the natural consequences of our behavior (Jer. 2:19)
- Through the wisdom and insight of others (Prov. 9:8–9)

The Father will correct you in wisdom and in love. He will "rightly correct you" (Jer. 46:28). Only a foolish child spurns her Father's discipline (Prov. 15:5). The prophetic charge against the city of Jerusalem was: "She has not obeyed His voice, She has not received correction; She has not trusted in the LORD, She has not drawn near to her God" (Zeph. 3:2).

How about you? Do you spurn the Father's correction? Do you fail to trust his love and his goodness? Do you suspect that he wishes to punish you harshly and do you harm? Do you run away rather than letting correction draw you closer to the Father's heart? Have you had faulty beliefs about the Father in this regard?

Close the chapter by submitting to the correction of the Father sent to Jerusalem through the prophet, Zephaniah. Pray and declare the following:

> *My dear Father, I will seek to walk in your way and obey your voice. I will gladly receive correction from your hand. I will trust in your goodness, your love, and your commitment to my well-being. I will draw near to you, my Father. Forgive me where I have failed to see aright. Guide me in your truth, and teach me. Amen.*

CHAPTER 21

THE FATHER IS PATIENT AND FORGIVING

My Dad was constantly angry. If I did something wrong, he would fume, rant, and rave. If I was late, if I misplaced something, if I made a mistake, he would be on my back like a hawk with talons extended. He was impatient with me. I can hardly remember a time when he wasn't stressed and angry about something. He rarely smiled. I continually sensed his displeasure, even when I wasn't doing anything wrong.

When I think of God the Father, I picture him as an angry judge. I feel like I need to perform and be as perfect as I can lest his anger be directed at me. In my head I know that he is also merciful and loving. But I feel these traits are a sort of anomaly, not in line with his basic character. To me the Father is the angry God who vengefully punishes sin and casts sinners into fiery torment, a totally fire-and-brimstone-type personality.

I hadn't really ever given much thought to how my concept of God the Father developed. In thinking about it, I can see that I have projected my experience with my earthly father on to my beliefs about the character of God.

—Joyce

The LORD is slow to anger, abounding in love and forgiving sin and rebellion. (Num. 14:18 NIV)

The Lord is not slow in keeping his promise, as some understand slowness. He is patient with you, not wanting anyone to perish, but everyone to come to repentance. (2 Pet. 3:9 NIV)

The LORD is compassionate and gracious,
slow to anger, abounding in love. . . .
He does not treat us as our sins deserve
or repay us according to our iniquities.
For as high as the heavens are above the earth,
so great is his love for those who fear him;
as far as the east is from the west,
so far has he removed our transgressions from us.
As a father has compassion on his children,
so the LORD has compassion on those who fear him.
(Ps. 103:8, 10–13 NIV)

Some years ago in a manufacturing town in Scotland, a young lady gathered a group of underprivileged children together for a Sunday school class. Because the children were so poorly dressed, the superintendent of the Sunday school invited them to come to his house during the week so he could outfit each child with a new suit of clothes for church.

The most poorly behaved and unpromising child in the class was a boy named Bob. After two or three Sundays, he stopped coming altogether. The teacher went out to look for him. He had been careless; his new suit was torn and dirty. But when she invited him back to class, he came.

The superintendent gave him a second new suit. However, after attending only one or two more times, he disappeared again. Once again the teacher sought him out, only to find that the second suit had gone the way of the first.

"I am utterly discouraged with Bob," she said when she reported the case to the superintendent. "I believe I am going to give up on him."

"Oh please, don't do that," the superintendent replied. "I can't help but hope there is a glimmer of promise in Bob. Let's try one more time. Tell him I'll give him a third suit if he'll promise to attend regularly."

Bob promised to attend and received his third new suit. He came regularly after that. Eventually he gave his life to Jesus and began to seek the Lord with his whole heart. The end of the story is that this forlorn, ragged, runaway boy became a great missionary to China.

Because the superintendent had patience and did not give up on him, Bob, whose full name is Robert Morrison, translated the Bible into the Chinese language and thus opened the kingdom of heaven to the millions of that vast country.

THE PATIENT FATHER

God is a patient father. The apostle Paul called him "the God of patience and comfort" (Rom. 15:5 KJV). He is "the compassionate and gracious God, slow to anger, abounding in love and faithfulness, maintaining love to thousands, and forgiving wickedness, rebellion and sin" (Exod. 34:6–7 NIV).

The word translated "slow to anger" can also be translated *longsuffering*. It means "to suffer long; to endure long before being angry; to wait expectantly and patiently." The Father has "enduring patience" (Jer. 15:15). Paul said that he is "rich" in tolerance and patience (Rom. 2:4 NIV).

The prophet Joel said "The LORD will be jealous for his land and take pity on his people" (Joel 2:18 NIV). The psalmist described God as "a compassionate and gracious God, slow to anger, abounding in love and faithfulness" (Ps. 86:15 NIV). Another psalm says, "The LORD is gracious and compassionate, slow to anger and rich in love. The LORD is good to all; he has compassion on all he has made" (Ps. 145:8–9 NIV).

Certainly these passages do not indicate that God is a pushover. He also punishes sin and disciplines those he loves. But even in discipline God remains patient and loving. Nehemiah extolled God's faithfulness. "They refused to listen and failed to remember the miracles you performed among them. They became stiff-necked and in their rebellion appointed a leader in order to return to their slavery. But you are a forgiving God, gracious and compassionate, slow to anger and abounding in love. Therefore you did not desert them" (Neh. 9:17 NIV).

Based on the verses above, would you agree with Joyce that the Father's basic disposition is anger? Did those who knew God in Old Testament times see the Father as impatient with his children? The answer to both these questions is a resounding no.

Since God was patient and loving even to his disobedient people, you and I can overcome the idea that the Father is impatient and angry. The phrase "slow to anger, abounding in love" occurs dozens of times throughout Scripture. The Bible teaches that the Father is patient with his children. His patience is big because his love is big.

HE IS PATIENT BECAUSE HE DESIRES VICTORY

Susanna Wesley, mother of John and Charles Wesley, was a patient woman. One time her husband said, "I marvel at your patience! You have told that child the same thing twenty times!"

Susanna looked fondly at her child and replied, "Had I spoken the matter only nineteen times, I should have lost all my labor."

This reminds me of an old saying: "Nothing is so full of victory as patience." Had Susanna been impatient rather than patient in raising her children, chances are that John and Charles would not have become such a spiritual force for renewal and revival in their generation. Patience makes way for victory.

Father God is patient with us because he desires that we experience victory in our lives. His rich tolerance and patience lead us to repentance (Rom. 2:4).

The book of 2 Peter deals with the judgment of God. Peter anticipated that some people would mistake the patience of God for a lack of willingness to act. In 2 Peter 3:9 he wrote: "The Lord is not slow in keeping his promise, as some understand slowness. He is patient with you, not wanting anyone to perish, but everyone to come to repentance" (NIV).

Possibly no passage in the New Testament more beautifully portrays God's patience than Luke 15:11–24. A son demanded his share of his inheritance, left home, and squandered his money in a far country. Not until poverty had reduced him to feeding pigs did the son confront reality. Finally he recognized the evil he had committed and returned to his father. The son expected to return as a slave, but his father welcomed him with forgiveness and acceptance.

The story of the prodigal son beautifully illustrates the Father heart of God. I want to draw your attention to several aspects of the Father's character in that parable.

1. The father loved his son enough to give him freedom.

When the son asked for his share of the estate, the father was under no obligation to give it. Furthermore, in Jewish tradition, fathers had authority to force their children to obey. Thus, the father could have easily disallowed his son from going.

In forcing obedience, the father may have kept his young son at home, but he would have lost his heart. By giving him what he wanted and allowing him to go, the father was creating the possibility for true relationship. The father gave his son freedom because he loved him. Although he was grieved at his son's departure, he was wise enough to wait until his son felt the need for a relationship with his father.

The father did not want outward conformity without heart relationship. And so he was willing to let go and wait. Our Father God desires a heart relationship with you. Like the waiting father in the story, God waits for you to respond to his great love.

2. The father watched patiently for his son to return.

The father knew that a relationship with his wayward son was not possible until his son had a change of heart. The son needed to reach a place of brokenness, sorrow, and humility. Every day the father stood at the end of the road and watched. Though he could have sent a servant to bring his son home, he did not. Daily he waited with patience and compassion for his son to come to his senses and return.

Have you sometimes wondered why God has not come and rescued you from some situation? I would not begin to lay down universal laws here. Scripture tells us that God is sovereign. Psalm 115:3 says, "Our God is in heaven; he does whatever pleases him" (NIV). We cannot say why God chooses to do the things he does, but could it be that we sometimes mistake his patience for a lack of concern?

3. The father completely and joyfully forgave.

The son eventually realized how foolish he had been. At the lowest point in his life, his thoughts returned to his father. He knew his father was kind and loving. Because of this, he decided to humble himself and return home. It was his father's kindness that led him to repentance.

When the father saw his tired, dirty, guilt-ridden son hesitantly coming down the road toward home, he joyfully ran toward him. With tears streaming down his face, the father embraced and kissed his son. There was no reserve or hesitation in his heart. There was no accusing or "I told you so." The father forgave instantly and completely.

The son recognized that he deserved to be demoted from the position of son to the position of servant, but the father would not hear of it. He cleaned him up, dressed him in fresh new clothes, and ordered the servants to prepare a great banquet.

Jesus told this story to teach about the father's heart. God is a waiting father. He does not condone sin and rebellion. He is grieved at how evil destroys us and others. But it is his love, his grief, his broken heart, and his willingness to wait and forgive that wins our hearts and draws us home.

In your relationship to the heavenly Father, where do you fall in the story of the prodigal son? Are you currently demanding your own way? Are you running away from him? After being away, are you now coming to your senses? Are you on the way home? Or are you in the Father's house, at his table?

Close the chapter by praying the following prayer, based on Psalm 103:8–13. If you have been wandering away from the Father, you may also want to spend some time "coming home" by confessing and repenting of your sins. The Father loves you. He is waiting for you to do so.

Dear Father, you are compassionate and gracious, slow to anger, abounding in love. You love me so much that you give me freedom to walk away and patiently wait for me to return home. And then you forgive. You do not treat me as my sins deserve or repay me according to my iniquities. For as high as the heavens are above the earth, so great is your love for me; as far as the east is from the west, so far have you removed my transgressions from me. You are my Father. I will love you forever. Amen.

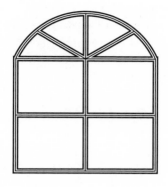

PART 5

Clearing the Barriers That Hinder Your Relationship with God the Father

Send forth your light and your truth,
let them guide me;
let them bring me to your holy mountain,
to the place where you dwell.
Then will I go to the altar of God,
to God, my joy and my delight.

—PSALM 43:3–4 NIV

The image of fatherhood that God gives in Jesus is a powerful one, but it does not automatically undo the damage of false fatherhood. Just knowing Christ does not rewire the very neural pathways of your brain. People are not changed by reading books on the New Testament doctrine of God's fatherhood. The new image that comes from Jesus has to penetrate to the deep subconscious springs of life and memory where the old images and reactions have their seat.

The Holy Spirit works in us to cry Abba, Father at precisely these deep places of our hearts and spirits. There the Spirit begins to transform us and set us free. Bit by bit He brings us out of the neglect or tyranny of the fatherhood we remember, into the sure love and liberating obedience of the God and Father of Jesus. At this point the great healer of the memories is the Spirit of the Son who spells out Father for us again and again till we are free of the old and believe the new.

—Thomas Smail[1]

CHAPTER 22

FATHER OF THE FATHERLESS

My mother was not married to my father. They lived together for a while, and then he moved out. My last contact with him was a card he sent for my birthday when I was three. I believe that not having a father in my life has affected me deeply. Like most girls, I became interested in boys in my early teens. But unlike the girls who had good fathers, I was terribly anxious and insecure around men. I was both fascinated and frightened by them. I craved male acceptance.

I gave up my virginity very early, within a few weeks of having a boyfriend, in hopes of winning a man's heart. With every boyfriend after that, and there were many, I wanted the relationship to go on forever. But they, like my father, just abandoned me and walked out of my life.

I am now twenty-five and starting to work through some of these issues. I fear betrayal, abandonment, and not being loved. I have a hard time with trust. I feel like I'm still a little girl inside, in desperate need of a daddy to affirm me. Right now I am trying to stay away from men in order to discover who my heavenly Father is. I need to be fathered. I need to be healed.

—*Laura*

When my father and my mother forsake me,
Then the LORD will take care of me. (Ps. 27:10)

A father to the fatherless, a defender of widows,
is God in his holy dwelling.
God sets the lonely in families,
he leads forth the prisoners with singing;
but the rebellious live in a sun-scorched land.
(Ps. 68:5–6 NIV)

The lone photo displayed on the shelf in her living room was of an aging man and woman. "Your parents?" I inquired. She nodded.

"It's hard to think about parents getting older," I commented. "I can't imagine what life would be like without them. . . . I'll miss mine very much."

She paused for a moment. "My father's dying won't make a difference to me," she said dryly. "In a way," she continued, "I am fatherless already, always have been."

Tonight about 40 percent of American children will go to sleep in homes in which their fathers do not live. And of those who are with their own fathers, many will fall asleep wondering if he actually wants to be with them.

Our society would have us believe that this really doesn't matter—that a mother, a caring environment, and perhaps an alternate father figure can easily make up for a father's absence. But our hearts and the multitudes of wounded flocking to the psychotherapist's couch tell us it is not so. Fathers matter. It is a fundamental cry of the human heart to be well fathered. It is a tragedy when any child is fatherless.

The care of the fatherless was a high priority for the Israelites. God strictly instructed his people to look out for their welfare. They were to protect their rights of inheritance, to invite them to share in the great annual feasts, and to give them a portion of the tithe crops (Exod. 22:22; Deut. 16:11, 14; 24:17; 26:12). The Father told the Israelites that he himself would take up the cause of the fatherless to work on their behalf (Deut. 10:18) and that anyone who failed to look out for their best interests would have to answer to him (Prov. 23:10).

Look at a few Scriptures that tell us what the Father promised to do for those who are fatherless:

> The LORD gives sight to the blind,
> the LORD lifts up those who are bowed down,
> the LORD loves the righteous.
> The LORD watches over the alien
> and sustains the fatherless and the widow,
> but he frustrates the ways of the wicked.
> (Ps. 146:8–9 NIV)

Do not take advantage of a widow or an orphan. If you do
and they cry out to me, I will certainly hear their cry.
(Exod. 22:22–23 NIV)

Do not move an ancient boundary stone
or encroach on the fields of the fatherless,
for their Defender is strong;
he will take up their case against you.
(Prov. 23:10–11 NIV)

Leave your orphans; I will protect their lives.
Your widows too can trust in me. (Jer. 49:11 NIV)

At the end of every three years, bring all the tithes of that
year's produce and store it in your towns, so that the Levites
(who have no allotment or inheritance of their own) and the
aliens, the fatherless and the widows who live in your towns
may come and eat and be satisfied, and so that the LORD your
God may bless you in all the work of your hands.
(Deut. 14:28–29 NIV)

If your earthly father died or abandoned you, you are well aware
of your fatherless condition. However, children who have fathers
involved in their lives may also experience a degree of fatherlessness.
Moreover, because no father can live up to the perfect fatherhood of
God, all of us are, in a certain sense, fatherless until we know him.

God is "a father to the fatherless" (Ps. 68:5 NIV). In him the fatherless find mercy (Hos. 14:3). Perhaps your experience with your earthly
father was not what it could have been. Perhaps you felt unloved,
rejected, embarrassed, or shamed. Perhaps you were ignored, pushed
aside, or even physically or sexually abused. Perhaps your father
struggled with addictions to drugs, alcohol, or gambling. Or perhaps
you were abandoned altogether.

Whatever type of parenting you experienced, your heavenly
Father can heal the places in which you are not whole. He is the perfect Father who desires to father his children perfectly. "When my
father and my mother forsake me, Then the LORD will take care of me"
(Ps. 27:10).

The following verses speak of how the Father helps the fatherless and how the fatherless can seek his help. Read the following verses and consider what they say about the Father.

> But You have seen, for You observe trouble and grief,
> To repay it by Your hand.
> The helpless commits himself to You;
> You are the helper of the fatherless. (Ps. 10:14)

> You hear, O Lord, the desire of the afflicted;
> you encourage them, and you listen to their cry,
> defending the fatherless and the oppressed,
> in order that man, who is of the earth, may terrify no more.
> (Ps. 10:17–18 niv)

> "For the oppression of the poor, for the sighing of the needy,
> Now I will arise," says the Lord;
> "I will set him in the safety for which he yearns."
> (Ps. 12:5)

I've taken the verses you just read and arranged their teaching in the form of a chart that outlines your responsibility and your heavenly Father's responsibility in dealing with the fatherlessness in your life.

The Father's Part

1. He knows the trouble and grief you have experienced.
2. He understands your heart's desire.
3. He encourages you to continue to seek his face.
4. He defends you so you can overcome your fear of man.
5. He helps you deal with your fatherlessness.
6. He sets you in the safe place you have been yearning for.

Your Part

1. Recognize your neediness.
2. Tell him about your struggles.
3. Cry out to the Father.
4. Take your tears and sighing to him.
5. Commit yourself to his fatherhood.

The Father wants to set you in the safe place you have been yearning for. Where is this safe place? Psalm 68:5 says God is "a father to the fatherless, a defender of widows, is God in his holy dwelling" (NIV). Verse 6 says, "God sets the lonely in families, he leads forth the prisoners with singing; but the rebellious live in a sun-scorched land" (NIV).

The phrase, "God sets the lonely in families," also can be translated, "God sets the desolate in a homeland." According to this passage, God is in his holy dwelling. He is in his home. And he wants to lead those who are lonely or desolate there. He wants to give them security. He wants to give them roots and a family identity, a land and a people they can call their own.

He wants them to know the truth about who their Father is and what he is like. The safe place is the place where he is. The place for which the needy yearn is the Father's house. The Father wants to bring you home.

The Father will lead you to his house with singing. But he will not force or coerce you to follow. The choice is yours. You can choose to be left behind, "imprisoned" in a "sun-scorched land" in bondage, desolate and tormented. Or you can allow him to free you and lead you to the safety, fellowship, and joy of his house.

Some people enjoy the misery of the wasteland. They want to hold on to their pain, resentment, and bitterness. They are unwilling to change, unwilling to move, unwilling to let go of the things that bind them. They do not want to take responsibility for their own attitudes and actions, preferring to blame others for the predicament they find themselves in. These people are unwilling to do what is necessary to enter into the intimacy of the Father's house.

In the coming chapters you will be identifying and clearing the barriers that hinder you from relating to God as Father. The Father will be faithful to do his part. He will help you overcome fear in order to bring you to the safety of his home. But you must do your part. You must recognize your neediness, take your fears and disappointments to him, and commit yourself to his fatherhood. You must be willing to leave the wasteland behind and follow the lead of the Father.

If you are able, signify your willingness to be led into the Father's house. Affirm each of the following statements that apply to you. Use the statements you choose as prayers to the Father. Pray to him and ask him to lead you to his home.

- I recognize that I do not always see the Father correctly. My life experiences and my own sin hinder me. I recognize that I am needy. I need and want a relationship with the Father. I need to know him. I want to grow in intimacy with him. I need his Spirit within me to cry out, "Abba, Father!" I want to be made increasingly aware of my deep need to know and relate to the Father in this way.

- Sometimes I struggle to relate to God as Father. I do not fully appreciate the beauty of the Father-daughter relationship. I am skeptical. I am afraid. I have many barriers in my heart. I wrap myself up in self-sufficiency and do not allow God to father me. But despite my struggles, I do want to know him as Father. I want to be able to appreciate the beauty of his fatherhood. I want to trust. I want to be able to pull down all barriers in order to be vulnerable to him.

- I commit myself to getting to know God as Father. Whatever it takes, I am willing to do it. I am willing to face my fear. I am willing to face my anger. I am willing to forgive. I am willing to repent. I am willing to be teachable. I am willing to be corrected with truth. I am willing to study and believe what the Bible says. I commit myself to seek to be free from all the thoughts and attitudes that would hinder my relationship with the Father. I recognize that he is my Father, and I give him permission to father me and lead me to his home.

CHAPTER 23

CONFRONTING FALSE BELIEFS ABOUT GOD THE FATHER

My perception of God the Father was one of a distant, loving, and judgmental God. These qualities were much the way my father was to me as I was growing up. My father was an alcoholic. This was how he chose to cope with having a large family and all the pressures that go along with that. He was distant emotionally. I always felt God the Father was the same. When God began to touch my heart at church during praise and worship—songs of God's great love for me—I was torn up inside because I wanted and needed God's love but could not trust it. I could not trust my own father to be there for me to support my emotional and spiritual needs at critical points in my life, so I couldn't trust Father God either. Thankfully, the Holy Spirit began to open up my heart to God's great love, so that the scar created by the relationship with my father was better understood and completely healed.

—Jennifer

Search me, O God, and know my heart;
Try me, and know my anxieties;
And see if there is any wicked way in me,
And lead me in the way everlasting. (Ps. 139:23–24)

Behold, You desire truth in the inward parts,
And in the hidden part You will make me to know
     wisdom.

Purge me with hyssop, and I shall be clean;
Wash me, and I shall be whiter than snow.
Make me hear joy and gladness. (Ps. 51:6–8)

We often go to my in-laws' cabin at a northern Canadian lake. It is beautiful there, peaceful and relaxing. I particularly enjoy watching the birds. There are hummingbirds, sparrows, wrens, pelicans, ducks, geese, and loons. A loon is a diving waterfowl with a sharp, pointed bill and a yodeling, laughter-like call. It hovers about fifteen feet above the water and then rapidly dives down below the surface to snatch fish.

When the children were young, they used to run on the pier. Tired of warning them not to run and not to go out so far, my husband called out, "Hey you kids, don't run out on the pier. And watch out for the loons; they hunt in pairs. They'll carry off small children that go too close to the edge."

As fate would have it, at that moment a loon cackled and dive-bombed down into the water just a few feet away from where the children were standing. Their eyes grew wide in terror, and they ran back to shore, screaming. Over the years it has become somewhat of a family joke. A child's dad, an uncle, or a grandpa will put on a worried look, shake his head gravely, and say, "Watch out for those loons. They hunt in pairs, you know, and carry off small children!"

It has been fascinating to watch how the children react. The young ones can be playing happily in the sand, but if they hear or see loons, they will jump up in fear and run to the safety of mom's arms. The children who are somewhat older suspect that the stories are a hoax. Grandma has repeatedly told them so. They have studied the loons a little and have not noticed any aggressive behavior toward humans. So when loons approach, they glance about nervously. They don't run away but are poised to do so, just in case the stories really are true.

The older children know that loons do not attack and would never hurt them. They like loons. It is fun to watch these graceful birds dive for fish. And they enjoy the joke. When they see loons, some of them will perpetuate the myth by urging the preschoolers to run and take cover. Other, more compassionate, less mischievous ones will try to reassure the young ones that there really is no danger.

The idea that loons attack and carry off children is a family myth. It is a myth the children learned from their fathers. Though untrue, belief in the myth causes the young ones to run away from loons. It is not until they mature and choose to believe the truth they hear from Grandma that they gain confidence in the character of loons and do not run away.

We often operate in a strikingly similar manner. We avoid God the Father because of our faulty beliefs about his character. However, as we discover and believe the truth and become more mature, our confidence in him increases.

Ephesians 4 tells us how God gave leaders for his church for the purpose of helping us to mature. Then verses 14 and 15 hold out a wonderful prospect. After we have grown up in Christ, "we will no longer be infants, tossed back and forth by the waves, and blown here and there by every wind of teaching and by the cunning and craftiness of men in their deceitful scheming. Instead, speaking the truth in love, we will in all things grow up into him who is the Head, that is, Christ" (Eph. 4:14–15 NIV).

Truth helps us grow up. That is why we need to pursue the truth. The children of Israel did not value truth in getting to know God. They were content to believe falsehood. Falsehood had become their "dwelling place."

"They are not valiant for the truth on the earth.
For they proceed from evil to evil,
And they do not know Me," says the LORD. . . .
"Your dwelling place is in the midst of deceit;
Through deceit they refuse to know Me," says the Lord.
(Jer. 9:3, 6)

When we do not pursue truth—being content, instead, to dwell in falsehood—we are, in essence, refusing to get to know God. In the process we put ourselves in danger of exchanging the truth about him for lies (Rom. 1:25). Satan is pleased when we do this. Satan does not hold "to the truth, for there is no truth in him. . . . he is a liar and the father of lies" (John 8:44 NIV). He wants us to believe lies about God the Father.

By contrast, the truth sheds light on falsehood. It exposes it (Eph. 5:8–13). In this book we have been looking at the truth about the fatherhood of God. Being equipped with truth, we can now look at our own beliefs and expose the areas in which we are dwelling in falsehood.

The chart below lists different types of earthly dads and how their behavior may have negatively influenced your perception of God the Father. Read through the list and identify any false perceptions and thoughts about Father God that you may have.

Type of Earthly Dad	Distorted Image of Father God
Absent Abandoning Dad	
This type of dad is absent. Whether through separation, divorce, death, travel, excess work, or any other reason, he is rarely, if ever, present.	• Father God will abandon me. • I do not trust Father God to be there when I need him. • Father God seems far away. • Father God will reject me.
Disinterested Dad	
Though present, this type of dad appears disinterested in his children. He rarely interacts with them and frequently misses games, concerts, birthdays, and other important events. Even when he is there, he's not really there; he's distracted with other things.	• Father God isn't concerned about the details of my life. • Father God has more important things to think about than me. • I'm afraid he's going to disappoint me. • He doesn't really care. • I'm not important enough to him to merit his attention.
Ticking-Time-Bomb Dad	
This dad is constantly on edge. He is irritable, angry, impatient, and moody. His children don't know why and constantly fear that they are doing something wrong.	• I feel uncomfortable in Father God's presence. He's an angry God. • Father God is impatient. • I feel as though I need to tiptoe around, pacify him, and appease his anger. • Father God is not pleased with me.

Drill-Sergeant Dad

Whenever this dad speaks, he barks out an order or command. All that his children know of him are his expectations of them.

- I feel I need to live up to God's expectations but fear that I won't.
- God will accept me only if I do everything he wants.
- The essence of my relationship with God is based on me following his rules.

Control-Freak Dad

This type of dad is manipulative and controlling. He does not allow his children freedom to make their own decisions and choices. He is overbearing and interfering.

- Father God takes pleasure in thwarting my plans.
- God is always breathing down my neck!
- I don't want to get close to Father God for fear of being smothered.
- Rules, rules, rules—that's all that a relationship with Father God is about.

Lecturing Dad

This type of dad is extremely opinionated. He is sure that he knows everything. He lectures his children incessantly. A favorite phrase of his is, "When I was a kid."

- Father God is extremely inflexible.
- His rules are stifling.
- Father God enjoys making me feel guilty about all my shortcomings and failures.
- His pleasure is based on my performance.

Heavy-handed Dad

A heavy-handed dad is punitive. His discipline is harsh and excessive. He punishes his children for childish mistakes. Spilled milk is a major offense.

- I am afraid that if I mess up, Father God is going to let the hammer fall.
- God is out to get me.
- He is punishing me.
- I'd better be good because he will really punish me if I'm not.

Abusive Dad

Physically and/or with words, this dad abuses his children. He physically injures them and/or screams at and belittles them and injures them emotionally.

- Father God is going to hurt me.
- Father God does not protect me.
- Father God does not love me.
- I am unacceptable to him.
- I deserve to be treated this way.

Stingy Scrooge Dad

A stingy scrooge dad is a poor provider. He is stingy and withholding toward his children. He resents spending money on them.

- Father God will not help me.
- I need to look out for myself.
- Father God takes some perverse pleasure in withholding good things from me.
- Father God enjoys watching me suffer.

Sugar Daddy Dad

Children know how to manipulate this type of dad. He gives his kids everything they ask for and does everything they want. His children are demanding and disrespectful.

- If he loved me, he would answer my prayers.
- I can make deals and bargains with God.
- If God doesn't do what I want, I'm going to give up on him.
- I just need to figure out the right formula to get Father God to do what I want.

Passive-Wimp Dad

This dad does not wear the pants in the house. He is passive and henpecked. He is cowardly and does not step up to defend his children when they feel threatened by outsiders.

- God can't protect me when others hurt me or when I'm in danger.
- I need to defend myself.
- I need to be independent because I can't rely on God.
- I'd better not put too much hope in him because he won't do anything for me.
- God is not really in control.

Impersonal Dad

An impersonal dad has difficulty expressing and receiving affection. Though he may love his children, he does not tell them that he loves them, nor does he physically display affection.

- God is awesome but not someone I can be close to.
- He is hidden and mysterious. I can't really get to know him.
- He cares about me but only from a distance.
- The thought of cuddling up in his lap is just weird.

Inconsistent Dad

He's unpredictable, one way today and a different way tomorrow. His children are cautious because they never know what kind of mood he'll be in.

- I can't depend on him.
- I'm afraid he's going to turn on me.
- I need to be cautious in my relationship with Father God.
- Father God might let me down.

Faultfinding Dad

Nothing a child does is ever good enough for a faultfinding dad. He is critical, blaming, and condemning.

- I can't live up to Father God's expectations.
- His love for me depends on my performance.
- I'm not good enough.
- I need to be perfect before I will win his wholehearted approval.
- He's not proud of me.

Guilt-Trip Dad

This type of dad is in the habit of using the phrase "after all I've done for you." He makes his kids feel like they owe him an enormous debt that they'd better pay up.

- I feel obligated to repay Father God for what he's done for me.
- God keeps a balance book with his deeds on one side and mine on the other. He expects my service as payment.
- I obey out of a sense of duty and debt.
- I constantly feel guilty that I'm not doing enough to please him.

Promise-breaking Dad

He makes promises but doesn't follow through. The promised outing never happens; the promised gift never materializes. His children expect him to disappoint them.

- Father God won't keep his promise.
- I'd better not get my hopes up because he'll disappoint me.
- His promises don't apply to me.
- I have to guard my heart so I won't be hurt.
- He doesn't really mean what he says.

Self-centered Dad

The universe revolves around this type of dad. Everything is about him. His children are only there to cater to his self-image and pleasure.

- Father God does what he wants without considering how it will affect me.
- He isn't interested in what I think.
- He doesn't listen to me when I pray.
- A relationship with Father God is one-sided. It's all about me serving him.

Hypocritical Dad

Dad doesn't practice what he preaches. He talks about purity but sneaks looks at dirty magazines. He talks about honesty but cheats on his tax return. He wants his children to be honest, but he tells lies.

- I have huge trust issues with Father God.
- I suspect that he is not really as good as he makes himself out to be.
- There is a dark side to Father God. I have suspicions about his true character.
- Father God confuses me. He expects me to be true, but he isn't true toward me.

Seducer-Abuser Dad

This type of dad seduces and abuses to satisfy his own perverted sexual needs. Coercion, shame, and secrecy are hallmarks of his relationship with his children.

- I am afraid of being abused by God.
- I cannot trust God since he let those horrible things happen to me.
- God doesn't love me.
- The only way to be safe is to keep my distance.

Dysfunctional Dad

Alcohol, drugs, gambling, sexual addictions, or psychological disorders are characteristic of the dysfunctional dad. He is unstable and often out of control. His children bear the brunt of his dysfunction.

- I have difficulty drawing near to Father God.
- I am afraid he will hurt me.
- I do not feel as though I can trust him.
- I seek to be in control. I can't rely on him to take care of me or heal me.
- Father God is unpredictable.
- I feel like I need to maintain a safe distance between him and me.

Did you identify with any of the false beliefs regarding God the Father? Perhaps you thought of others that weren't on the list. Or perhaps in reading through the list, you recognized that your image of Father God was not negatively influenced by your earthly father. In any case it is beneficial to examine our thoughts and assumptions about God the Father and to counter and correct any false beliefs we discover. We all have areas in which we can grow in our understanding of him.

The following list records the truths about God the Father we have considered in the previous chapters of this book. Think about each statement carefully. Give yourself a score of zero to five for each statement. Five means "I live as though I totally believe this statement." Zero means "I live as though I totally disbelieve this statement." Evaluate the extent to which you believe or disbelieve each truth. Do not merely consider whether you intellectually assent to it. Instead, take a look at your life to determine whether you live as though you believe it. Before you begin, pray and ask the Father to search your heart and have the Holy Spirit enable you honestly to evaluate what you believe.

_____ My Father wants a close relationship with me.

_____ My Father loves me with an everlasting love.

_____ My Father lavishes his love upon me.

_____ My Father is kind and gentle toward me.

_____ My Father is always with me.

_____ My Father is my friend.

_____ My Father looks after me.

_____ My Father is strong and powerful.

_____ My Father uses his strength to help me.

_____ My Father protects me.

_____ My Father will use affliction for good purposes in my life.

_____ As I ask, my Father will provide everything I need.

_____ My Father is devoted to me.

_____ My Father delights in me.

_____ My Father is totally dependable.

_____ My Father gives me perfect guidance.

_____ My Father's correction is loving and good.

_____ My Father is patient with me and forgives me.

Now add up your score. It will range from between zero and ninety: ninety being total belief and zero being total disbelief. If you were honest, you probably did not get a score of ninety. I do not believe that, while we are in this present world, any of us live as though we absolutely believe the truths about the Father. But knowing him in a relationship of truth ought to be our continual focus and goal. Having eternal life means getting to know the Father better (John 17:3).

To close this chapter, review each area in which you dwell in falsehood. Talk to the Father about each one. Ask him to forgive you, to cleanse you, and to give you the Spirit of wisdom and revelation so that you can know him better.

> I keep asking that the God of our Lord Jesus Christ, the glorious Father, may give you the Spirit of wisdom and revelation, so that you may know him better. (Eph. 1:17 NIV)

CHAPTER 24

CHOOSING TO BELIEVE THE TRUTH ABOUT GOD THE FATHER

Even though we tend to do so, we cannot base our perceptions of God and our feelings about ourselves on how we were treated by our parents. Fathers and mothers are human and fallible—and some of them are even prodigals! Our beliefs based on childhood experiences need to be cleaned out of our minds and emotions and replaced with accurate beliefs about God based on His Word. You need to transfer the basis of your identity from your fallible father to your infallible heavenly Father. . . .

It's so easy to hold God responsible for our problems and how we feel about ourselves. But God is not the problem. Rather, it's our mistaken perceptions of Him that block the reality of who He really is.

—H. Norman Wright[1]

Keep me from deceitful ways;
be gracious to me through your law.
I have chosen the way of truth;
I have set my heart on your laws. (Ps. 119:29–30 NIV)

Sanctify them by Your truth. Your word is truth.
(John 17:17)

The LORD is near to all who call upon Him,
To all who call upon Him in truth. (Ps. 145:18)

FASTEN THE BELT OF TRUTH

Keep one thing forever in view—truth; and if you do this,
though it may seem to lead you away from the opinion of men,
it will assuredly conduct you to the throne of God.

—HORACE MANN (1796–1859)

Roman soldiers wore tunics made of a large, square piece of material with holes cut out for the head and arms. Normally the tunic draped loosely around the body. But in battle, a loose tunic would be a potential danger. Therefore, when preparing for battle, the soldier would gather up his tunic and tuck it securely under the wide, heavy leather belt strapped around his lower back (over his loin muscles).

The belt kept everything in its proper place. Without it the soldier's sword and other weapons would be inaccessible. Furthermore, his loose tunic would impede him and make him vulnerable to deadly entanglements.

An essential part of the Christian's spiritual armor is the belt of truth (Eph. 6:14). Paul instructs believers to stand firm with the belt of truth buckled around their waists. He urges them to prepare themselves by "girding up their waist," which means tucking all the loose parts of the tunic into the belt.

Truth is the belt that holds the parts of the Christian armor together. It binds up thoughts and attitudes that can impede or perhaps even endanger us. It holds the scabbard for the sword of the Spirit, which is the Word of God. Without the belt of truth, we are spiritually hindered, ineffective, and endangered.

First Peter 1:13 says, "Therefore gird up the loins of your mind." Based on Paul's analogy of the Roman soldier, we spiritually prepare for battle by getting the truth solidly and deeply into our minds. To be prepared for battle, we need to tuck the "loose" parts of our minds into the belt of truth. We need to take our false attitudes and beliefs about the Father and bind them up with truth so that they will not hinder us.

The process Peter and Paul described requires a conscious decision followed by a continual process. The apostle Paul said it requires that we take every thought captive:

> The weapons we fight with are not the weapons of the world. On the contrary, they have divine power to demolish strongholds. We demolish arguments and every pretension that sets itself up against the knowledge of God, and we take captive every thought to make it obedient to Christ. (2 Cor. 10:4–5 NIV)

I reworded the teachings of those verses into the words of the following statement:

> The belt of truth and the sword of Scripture destroy every false argument and every pretentious thought that would keep me from knowing God my Father. These weapons have divine power to tear down strongholds in my life. Victory in this battle demands that I continually "gird up" my mind by capturing each false thought and making it obedient to Jesus.

The Father does not force us to comply with truth. It is our choice. He does not want mechanical obedience. He wants our hearts. He wants us to love truth (Zech. 8:19; 2 Thess. 2:10), to seep our inward parts with truth (Ps. 51:6), and to walk faithfully in truth (2 John 4; 3 John 3–4).

The Father wants us to desire truth so much that we plead for it (Isa. 59:4). King David begged him, "Show me your ways, O LORD, teach me your paths; guide me in your truth and teach me, for you are God my Savior, and my hope is in you all day long" (Ps. 25:4–5 NIV).

BUY THE TRUTH

How can you know truth? According to Scripture, the Father is truth (Ps. 31:3–5; John 8:26), what the Father says is truth (John 17:17; Ps. 119:160), the Father's only Son is truth (John 14:6), the Spirit that comes from the Father is truth (John 14:17), and Scripture is truth

(Phil. 4:8). Knowing truth means knowing the Father, the Son, and the Spirit. It means studying and believing the truth that is revealed in the Bible.

King Solomon told his children to "buy the truth and do not sell it; get wisdom, discipline and understanding" (Prov. 23:23 NIV). Solomon realized that it takes some effort to acquire truth. Truth costs.

Here are some of ways we can "buy" truth:

1. Read the Bible.

Blessed is the one who reads the words of this prophecy, and blessed are those who hear it and take to heart what is written in it, because the time is near. (Rev. 1:3 NIV)

2. Learn how to handle Scripture correctly.

All Scripture is God-breathed and is useful for teaching, rebuking, correcting and training in righteousness. (2 Tim. 3:16 NIV)

3. Memorize and quote Scripture.

I have hidden your word in my heart
that I might not sin against you.
Praise be to you, O LORD;
teach me your decrees.
With my lips I recount
all the laws that come from your mouth.
(Ps. 119:11–13 NIV)

4. Spend time thinking and meditating on truth.

Finally, brothers, whatever is true, whatever is noble, whatever is right, whatever is pure, whatever is lovely, whatever is admirable—if anything is excellent or praiseworthy—think about such things. (Phil. 4:8 NIV)

5. Identify and repent of all falsehood.

Surely I was sinful at birth,
sinful from the time my mother conceived me.
Surely you desire truth in the inner parts;
you teach me wisdom in the inmost place.

Cleanse me with hyssop, and I will be clean;
wash me, and I will be whiter than snow.
(Ps. 51:5–7 NIV)

6. Speak the truth to others and listen when they speak truth to
   you.

Therefore each of you must put off falsehood and speak truthfully to his neighbor, for we are all members of one body.
(Eph. 4:25)

Knowing Scripture is our most powerful weapon of truth. Martin
Luther, the great German reformer, had memorized virtually all of the
Bible. Charles Wesley, a powerful evangelist, had memorized most of
the Greek New Testament. That's what enabled these men to discern
truths about God. For you to stop dwelling in falsehood and to mature
in your relationship with the Father, you need to read the Word, meditate on the Word, memorize the Word, and bring every one of your
thoughts under the authority of the Word.

Have you memorized a verse of Scripture that will help you bind
your false thoughts under the belt of truth? Do you think and meditate on this Scripture continually?

If you have not committed an applicable verse to memory, go back
to the section of this book that applies to your struggle and select a
verse of Scripture. Memorize it. Think and meditate on it constantly.
If you do so, I can guarantee that your thoughts about the Father will
begin to change. And as you "buy truth" (Prov. 23:23) by making a
habit of hiding more and more of God's Word in your heart, you will
see falsehood slowly die by the sword of the Spirit.

Truth Leads to the Father's House

In the following verses, look for the phrases that indicate the
place where truth leads.

Send forth your light and your truth,
let them guide me;
let them bring me to your holy mountain,
to the place where you dwell.

Then will I go to the altar of God,
to God, my joy and my delight. (Ps. 43:3–4 NIV)

"If you abide in My word, you are My disciples indeed. And
you shall know the truth, and the truth shall make you
free. . . . Most assuredly, I say to you, whoever commits sin is a
slave of sin. And a slave does not abide in the house forever,
but a son abides forever." (John 8:31, 31–32, 34–35)

Truth leads to the place where God dwells. It guides us away from
dwelling in falsehood and takes us toward the Father's house. His
house is the house of truth. His city is the city of truth (Zech. 8:3).
With truth we gain freedom to enter the presence of the Father. And
through truth he becomes our joy and delight.

Psalm 145:18 says, "The LORD is near to all who call upon Him,
to all who call upon Him in truth." As a fellow traveler on this journey, may I challenge you to make a commitment to call on the Father
in truth. Pray and ask God for guidance, then make a specific plan to
"buy" truth. Here are some examples of the kind of specific plans
I mean:

- I will buy a book on the names of God and study one of his
  names each day.
- I will look up all the verses about the faithfulness of God in a
  concordance.
- I will memorize Jeremiah 31:3 and meditate on the Father's love
  for me.

Some will have more trouble than others in overcoming false
beliefs about Father God. Perhaps you will be able to take only one
small step at a time. But if you take the risk to believe the truth, I guarantee that you will be drawn toward, delight in, and be made whole by
the love of your perfect heavenly Father. In him you will find the
father of your dreams!

CHAPTER 25

MAKING PEACE WITH YOUR EARTHLY FATHER: FORGIVENESS

Dad was strict and sometimes even harsh. As a child, I was afraid of him. He didn't speak much, so I never felt that I knew him well. As an adult, I had to come to the place of realizing that my heavenly Father was not going to crush me every time I did something wrong. I also had to recognize that he wanted to be close to me.

There were some things I needed to forgive my own dad for in order for this to happen. I had to forgive dad for the times he disciplined me when I was not guilty of any wrongdoing. I had to forgive him for being disappointed that I was a girl and not a boy. I had to let go of my bitterness and the feelings that I could never live up to his expectations.

There were also some things about Dad that in my childishness I had misinterpreted. Being self-employed, Dad worked extremely long hours. As a child, I interpreted his lack of time for me as not wanting to be with me. As an adult, however, I realize that he worked out of necessity. But even though my perception was immature, I carried it into adulthood and projected it onto my relationship with my dad and with God.

Now that I am an adult, the responsibility for all these things rests on my shoulders. I can choose to live with faulty beliefs about the Father, or I can correct them. Also, I have the choice to live status quo in my relationship with Dad, or I can let the heavenly Father pour healing into me so that I can reach out to Dad and have a better relationship with him too.

The freedom of all this is amazing. Instead of personalizing everything Dad does or says, I am able to realize that he has areas where he needs to be touched by the Father. And I am able to interact with him with compassion. In doing so, I am finding that my relationship with both my earthly and my heavenly Father is more than I had ever thought possible.

—*Debbie*

Therefore, as the elect of God, holy and beloved, put on tender mercies, kindness, humility, meekness, longsuffering; bearing with one another, and forgiving one another, if anyone has a complaint against another; even as Christ forgave you, so you also must do. But above all these things put on love, which is the bond of perfection. (Col. 3:12–14)

And above all things have fervent love for one another, for "love will cover a multitude of sins." (1 Pet. 4:8)

Therefore confess your sins to each other and pray for each other so that you may be healed. The prayer of a righteous man is powerful and effective. (James 5:16 NIV)

When thou forgivest, the man who has pierced thy heart stands to thee in the relation of the sea-worm, that perforates the shell of the mussel, which straightway closes the wound with a pearl.

—JEAN PAUL RICHTER (1763–1825)

May I tell you why it seems to me a good thing for us to remember wrong that has been done us? That we may forgive it.

—CHARLES DICKENS (1812–1870)

In the previous chapter we examined the fact that that truth leads to the Father's house. But even though Christians may be exposed to truth, some are still unable to believe it. This was a problem that Paul warned Timothy about. He said that there would be persons whose wills were so weakened by sin that though they heard truth, they would be unable to accept it. They would be "always learning and never able to come to the knowledge of the truth" (2 Tim. 3:7). Sin, when not dealt with, cripples the will so that a person is unable to choose truth and enter the Father's house.

According to Paul, we may become "loaded down" with sin. The phrase "loaded down" means "to heap up, or to stack up continually so as to increase one's burden." Sin that stacks up over a period of time makes us vulnerable to falsehood and deception.

In the father-child relationship, a child is vulnerable to the sins of unforgiveness, resentment, and bitterness. Because his father is such an important person in his life, he clearly remembers the things his father does and doesn't do. He takes the real or perceived failure to heart. And in his pain and disappointment, he covers each incident with a layer of self-justified resentment. Over the years layer upon layer of unforgiveness stacks up. Eventually, he may reach adulthood and find that he is like the beautiful princess on top of hundreds of mattresses, unable to rest because the green pea underneath is making him black and blue.

Now I want to ask you to undertake a serious challenge. I want to ask you to identify areas in which the fathering you received was contrary to the Fatherhood of God. If possible, you will clear sin out of your life by forgiving your father for these things. In the next chapter I will ask you to think of ways your father blessed you with positive examples of fatherhood. In this chapter, however, you will only be looking at fathering incidents that you perceive as negative.

There are a few points that you should be aware of before you begin. First, your perceptions about your father's character or motivation may be accurate or inaccurate. It is interesting that two children growing up together with the same father can have different perceptions of him. How we read our fathers depends on many factors such as our birth order, gender, age, personality, and insight into his circumstances. I'll never forget the time my brothers and I were discussing our memories of our grandfather. I remembered him as playful and kind, while my brothers remembered him as strict and harsh. It didn't seem possible that we were talking about the same person! The ways we perceived him were so different!

Keep this in mind when you consider your thoughts about your dad. I want you to recognize that you are merely considering your own perceptions of the fathering you received. Whether your perceptions are correct or incorrect is not the issue. You are examining them in order to clear the barriers in your heart that would hinder you in responding to the fatherhood of God. Please realize that you are not doing this to find fault with or lay blame on your earthly father.

This brings me to a second point. As an adult you are responsible for the attitudes in your heart. Although your father and others may have sinned against you, your attitude is your own responsibility. Perhaps you were unable to control what happened, but you are able to choose how you will respond. You may choose to forgive. Or you may choose to let resentment and bitterness continue to stack up in your life, making you vulnerable to deception and unable to enter the Father's house. The choice is yours.

Finally, if your experience with your father was extremely damaging, in instances of incest, sexual abuse, or addictive behavior, for example, you may need additional counseling to reach a place of healing and forgiveness. Please do not hesitate to seek help.

The following steps of forgiveness are intended to help you clear the barriers that hinder you in relating to God as Father. To begin, I would like you to identify things in your relationship with your father that you wish could have been different.

STEP 1. IDENTIFY THE AREAS IN WHICH YOU PERCEIVE LOSS OR INJURY

Get some blank paper or your journal. Begin to write your responses to these questions. You could just think about these issues, but many people testify to the fact that writing down their thoughts multiplies the effectiveness of the exercise. Include general themes and specific instances. For example, you might write down something like this: "Dad, I wish that you would have spent more time with me," or, "Dad, I wish you would have congratulated me when I made the honor roll," or, "Dad, I wish you would not have been unfaithful to Mom." Write down everything that comes to mind, no matter how insignificant it may seem. Spend some time on this.

a. What do you wish had happened with your father that didn't happen?

b. What are some things that he did that you wish he hadn't done?

Step 2. Identify the Effects These Experiences Have Had on Your Life

Next, try to identify how these experiences have affected your perception of yourself (for example, "I feel that I am unworthy of being loved." "I feel incompetent." "I feel insecure." "I feel angry, humiliated, guilty, ashamed, sad, or betrayed.") as well as your perception of God the Father ("I feel that God the Father could not possibly love me." "I feel that God the Father is out to get me.").

    a. How have these experiences affected your perception of yourself?

    b. How have these experiences affected your perception of Father God?

Step 3. Make the Decision to Forgive Your Father

Write him a letter.

Write a letter to your father, forgiving him for the things you just identified. (You will not be giving this letter to him.) Recognize that forgiving is not a feeling but a decision. Many people have serious and sometimes even criminal complaints toward their parents. But holding on to bitterness does nothing but prolong the pain. Your bitterness and resentment toward your dad does far more damage to you than it does to him. I am challenging you to do the work described. Your feelings will follow the choices you make and act upon.

- Address the letter to your father: "Dear Dad."
- Express your choice to forgive him for the items you listed in step 1. List each one specifically: "Dad, I forgive you for blaming me for stealing money out of your wallet when I really didn't do it." "Dad, I forgive you for choosing to read the newspaper instead of spending time with me." "Dad, I forgive you for making fun of my developing body."
- Tell him how these things have affected you. List all the things you wrote in step 2. "Because of the way you fathered me, I feel. . . ." Include how his fathering has affected your feelings about yourself as well as how it has affected your feelings about the fatherhood of God.

- Recognize that he also needs fathering and release him from the responsibility of being a perfect father to you: "Dad, I realize that there are areas in your life in which you also need fathering. Only God is the perfect Father, so I release you from the responsibility of being a perfect father to me. I forgive you and release you totally and completely."
- Close and sign the letter.

Read the letter to a trusted friend.

Sharing what you have written is an important step. The apostle Paul said that we should confess our sins to one another and pray for one another that we might be healed (James 5:16). Read the letter aloud to your friend. Ask him or her to pray for you so that you might completely forgive and release your father from the debt of fathering he owes you. Also have him or her pray for your healing in this area. If you are unable to read the letter to a friend, read it out loud to an empty chair.

Cancel the debt.

Cancel the debt of fathering your father owes you by writing *canceled* in large letters across the page(s). Then burn the letter or rip it into small pieces and throw it away.

STEP 4. REMEMBER THAT THE DEBT HAS BEEN CANCELED

Each month for many years I wrote a check to the bank for the mortgage payment on our house. When we saved up enough money, we paid out our debt and canceled the mortgage. But the next month, when the usual time for payment came, through force of habit, I began to write another check. I stopped in midstream when I remembered that I didn't have to pay that bill anymore. The internal prompting to write a check came back again the next month and for a few months after that. Every month I reminded myself that the title on our house was clear. Gradually the urge lessened and finally ceased.

Forgiveness and truth work the same way. The transaction of forgiveness is complete, but it may take a while for your old habits of thought to be replaced with new ones. This is why it is important that you discipline yourself and "take captive every thought" (2 Cor. 10:5 NIV).

Whenever you have a thought that goes contrary to what you have decided and what you know to be true, you must grasp it and firmly tuck it under your belt of truth. You must do this with every thought of resentment against your earthly father, with every wrong thought about yourself, and with every falsehood about the fatherhood of God. As you continually remind yourself of truth, wrong thoughts will gradually lessen and cease.

Through forgiveness, you buy truth. It is yours. You own it. You may keep it or sell it. The choice is yours. Keeping it means controlling false thoughts by taking every one of them captive. Selling it means letting wrong thoughts control you. Solomon advised, "Buy the truth and do not sell it; get wisdom, discipline and understanding" (Prov. 23:23 NIV).

Falsehood will keep you captive. Truth will set you free. If you follow, it will lead you to the Father's house. And in his presence you will be free indeed.

CHAPTER 26

MAKING PEACE WITH OUR EARTHLY FATHERS: BLESSING

Dad came to every one of my track meets. As I prepared, I would search the stands for his face, just to make sure he was there. It was his cheers I heard when I crossed the finish line. And once, when I fell and badly sprained my ankle in the middle of a race, it was he who bolted out of the stands, carried me gently to the car, and drove me to the medical center.

When we got home, he prepared the pack of ice as I lay on the couch. Then he waited on me all evening: he changed ice packs, brought me supper, gave me painkillers, adjusted the couch so I could see the TV, and sat with me to keep me company. At night he carried me upstairs to my room, tucked me into bed, and gave me a kiss on the forehead.

"Just call if you need me. You know I'll be there," he whispered. I had no doubt. He always was. The next morning I discovered that he had pulled out a sleeping bag and slept on the floor on the landing, just so he could be close enough to my room to hear if I called.

This example tells you about the loving, wonderful part of my dad. But it doesn't tell the whole story. Dad wasn't perfect; his Irish temper often got the best of him. And he sometimes did and said things that hurt me.

But I do not like to focus on the negative. It has been forgiven. I like to focus on the good in Dad, for those traits are like my heavenly Father's. Despite some shortcomings, my dad gave me a solid foundation from which to trust and want to get to know God as Father.

—Bonnie

"Honor your father and mother," which is the first command-
ment with promise: "that it may be well with you and you may
live long on the earth." (Eph. 6:2–3)

In the previous chapter you identified areas in which you perceived loss or injury in your experience with your earthly father. You
did this to clear any barriers of sin in your life that may have been pre-
venting you from seeing God the Father correctly. You did not do this
to judge or condemn your father. That is not your place.

The Bible is clear on the responsibility of children toward parents.
As young children, we are to obey our parents (Eph. 6:1). But our
responsibility toward our parents does not cease when we are grown.
Throughout life we are to respect and honor them.

To *honor,* means "to deem or hold worthy, to recognize, to praise."
To honor one's parents means to recognize their contribution to our
lives, to hold them worthy, to praise them, to care about them and for
them.

Honoring one's parents is not an option. It is a command. It was
included in the Ten Commandments (Exod. 20:12). The Israelites
took this command so seriously that they punished violence against
parents (physically striking or verbally cursing them) by putting the
offending child to death (Exod. 21:15, 17).

Honoring parents was the first command that had a promise
attached to it. God said that it would "be well" with children who honored their parents and that he would reward this behavior by granting
children who did this an increased life span (Eph. 6:2–3). Therefore,
honoring our parents not only benefits our parents; it also benefits us.
When we honor them, our lives go much better than when we do not.

Honoring our fathers is one of the basic ways in which we put our
religion into practice (1 Tim. 5:4). According to the Bible, a father
does not need to be good in order to receive honor from his daughter
or son. Whether he is a good or bad father is not the issue. The godly
child gives him honor simply because he is her father and because
doing so is right in the eyes of God.

The following verses illustrate how, as an adult, you can honor
your father. I honor my father by:
- Caring for him, being involved in his life (1 Tim. 5:4)
- Bringing him joy (Prov. 10:1; 27:11)
- Being his "crown" (Prov. 17:6)

- Being his delight and bringing him gladness (Prov. 23:22–25)
- Being concerned about his well-being (1 Tim. 5:4)
- Providing for his needs (Matt. 15:5)
- Speaking well of him (Exod. 21:17)

Relating to your earthly father by honoring him will help clear barriers that hinder your relationship to Father God. In this chapter I will encourage you to honor your earthly father by identifying the positive contributions he has made to your life. I will then encourage you to write a letter, thanking him for these contributions.

STEP 1. IDENTIFY THE WAYS YOUR FATHER HAS BLESSED YOU

Your father has blessed you. At the very least he has blessed you by giving you life. Quite likely he has blessed you in many other significant ways. If you had a father who failed in major and possibly tragic ways, you can still honestly recognize the positive elements among the broken pieces.

Here is a list of ways fathers add to or care for their children's lives.

Mentally check each way in which your father has contributed to your life. If your father was particularly dysfunctional, you may want to add a percentage of the time to your responses. Don't allow the areas where your father was unable or unwilling to act responsibly blind you to his positive contributions.

My dad:
- Gave me life.
- Was present (at least some of the time).
- Loved my mom.
- Was the leader of our family.
- Was concerned about my well-being.
- Was strong.
- Provided financially for me.
- Protected me.
- Taught and guided me.
- Corrected my faulty behavior.
- Loved me.
- Affirmed my femininity/masculinity.

My dad modeled or taught the following values:
- The importance of God
- The importance of family
- The importance of others
- The eternal significance of one's earthly life
- A sense of right and wrong
- Faithfulness to commitments
- Integrity
- Dedication
- Stability
- Responsibility
- Self-discipline
- Self-control
- Respect for authority
- The importance of hard work
- A sense of duty
- The value of play and relaxation
- The value of learning and education
- The value of self-improvement
- Interpersonal communication
- Giving your best effort
- Completing what you start
- Courage
- Honesty
- A sense of fairness
- A sense of humor
- Forgiveness
- Kindness
- Enthusiasm for life
- Friendship
- Friendliness
- Love
- Compassion
- Loyalty
- Generosity
- Helpfulness
- Service
- Moral fidelity and purity

- Encouragement
- Patience
- Sensitivity
- Being considerate of others
- Wisdom
- Humility
- Creativity
- Approachability
- Physical fitness
- Organization
- Planning ahead
- Love of country
- Civic responsibility
- Community involvement
- Financial responsibility

Also think of any other positive values your father modeled or taught you.

Skills My Dad Taught Me

Think of specific skills your father taught you. Did he teach you how to fish, how to balance a checkbook, how to ride a bike, how to change the oil in the car, how to mow the lawn, how to play chess, how to garden, how to use an encyclopedia, how to play football, or how do algebra? You might want to jot these down as well.

STEP 2. WRITE YOUR FATHER A LETTER

In a letter express gratitude for the contributions your father has made to your life. Psalm 92:1 says that it is good to give thanks to your heavenly Father. It is also good to give thanks to your earthly father. It honors him. Recognizing the contributions he made to your life does not mean that you endorse all of his behavior (for example, saying you appreciate him teaching you how to ride your bike does not mean that you appreciated him losing his temper), but it does express gratitude and give honor where honor is due.

On a separate sheet of paper, write a letter to your father recognizing and thanking him for all of the positive contributions he made to your life.

The goal of this letter is to bless and honor your father, not to correct or rebuke him.

- Do not speak of the negative, only the positive.
- Refer to the above lists for specific items to mention.
- Thank him for being your father.
- Thank him, if you are able, for the good things he taught you about the fatherhood of God.

Have a friend proofread your letter to ensure that it is positive and does not have any negative undertones. If necessary, rewrite it.

STEP 3. GIVE THE LETTER TO YOUR FATHER

When the letter is completed to your satisfaction, read, give, or send it to your father. If your father has died or you do not know his whereabouts, this may not be possible. Also, if you have been sexually abused by your father, postpone sending a letter until you have adequately dealt with your pain and with issues of healing and forgiveness. You may want to ask a Christian counselor for advice before sending this letter to him.

If you are in contact with your father, are not a victim of sexual abuse, but are hesitant to send him such a letter, ask yourself why. Are you afraid of his reaction? Are you too proud? Do you still hold resentments? Do you hesitate to bless him because you want to see him suffer? Do you withhold blessing from him because he withheld it from you? Be honest with yourself. Remember, evil is not overcome by evil but by good (Rom. 12:21).

Elisabeth Elliott once said, "It is always possible to be thankful for what is given rather than resentful for what is not. One or the other becomes a way of life."

Which way of life will you choose with regard to your father? Will you be thankful for what you received from him or resentful for what you did not?

Close this section by praying and asking the Father to help you honor your earthly father in a way that ultimately brings honor to God.

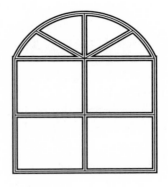

PART 6

In My Father's House

*One thing I have desired of the L*ORD,
That will I seek:
*That I may dwell in the house of the L*ORD
All the days of my life,
*To behold the beauty of the L*ORD,
and to inquire in His temple.

—PSALM 27:4

The experience of heaven will be a family gathering, as the great host of the redeemed meet together in face-to-face fellowship with their Father-God and Jesus their brother. This is the deepest and clearest idea of heaven that the Bible gives us. . . .

It will be like the day when the sick child is at last able to leave the hospital and finds his father and the whole family waiting there to greet him—a family occasion, if ever there was one. "I see myself now at the end of my journey," said Bunyan's Mr. Stand-fast, as he stood halfway into Jordan's water. "The thoughts of what I am going to, and of the conduct that waits for me on the other side, doth lie as a glowing coal at my heart. . . . I have formerly lived by hearsay and faith, but now I go where I shall live by sight, and shall be with him in whose company I delight myself."

What will make heaven heaven is the presence of Jesus and a reconciled divine Father who loves us for Jesus' sake no less than he loves Jesus himself. To see and know and love and be loved by the Father and the Son, in company with the rest of God's vast family, is the whole essence of the Christian hope. If you are a believer, and so a son or daughter, this prospect satisfies you completely. If it does not strike you as satisfying, it would seem that as yet you are neither.

—J. I. Packer[1]

CHAPTER 27

MY FATHER'S HOUSE

My father never gave advice, unless you asked for it of course. Even then it was more apt to be given in a story. My dad was a great storyteller—stories of his life growing up as a farm boy in southern Saskatchewan, his job with the railway on the wrecking crane, and finally as a cab driver in the Okanagan. But the one thing I remember him always saying is this: "You know you always have a home here to come to." All through my life, no matter what mistakes I made, at every low point in my life, I knew that if life got too much to handle I could always go home.

—Sharon

I love the house where you live, O LORD,
the place where your glory dwells. (Ps. 26:8 NIV)

They feast on the abundance of your house;
you give them drink from your river of delights.
For with you is the fountain of life;
in your light we see light. (Ps. 36:8–9 NIV)

The righteous will flourish like a palm tree,
they will grow like a cedar of Lebanon;
planted in the house of the LORD,
they will flourish in the courts of our God.
They will still bear fruit in old age,
they will stay fresh and green. (Ps. 92:12–14 NIV)

But I am like an olive tree
flourishing in the house of God. (Ps. 52:8 NIV)

I was glad when they said to me, "Let us go into the house of the LORD." (Ps. 122:1)

Close your eyes and imagine your dream home. What is it like? Is it a country plantation? A log cabin in the mountains? A Mediterranean villa? A sprawling ranch house? An urban penthouse condominium? A cottage? A conservatory? A palatial mansion? The possibilities go on and on.

Archeologists have determined that wealthy people during the time of Christ lived in houses that consisted of a series of rooms arranged around a covered or partially covered central courtyard. The courtyard was the family gathering place and the place for food storage and preparation. It contained an oven, a mill for grinding grain, storage jars for food, a large stone mortar and pestle, as well as a table and eating utensils.

The word *house* is an important word in the Bible. It is used more than two thousand times in the Old Testament alone. When used, it has three basic meanings: The first and most obvious meaning is that of a physical structure where someone lives. It can refer to all kinds of dwellings from palaces (Jer. 39:8) and temples (1 Kings 8:13) to private houses (Exod. 12:7) and even tents (Gen. 33:17–18).

The word *house* also is used to signify a family line of ancestry. "House of Israel" refers to all of Jacob's descendants, the members of the Jewish nation (Exod. 40:38). Jacob's twelve sons had an emblem that represented their own houses (Num. 2:2): the house of Levi (Exod. 2:1), the house of Joseph (Gen. 50:8), and the house of Judah (2 Sam. 2:10) for example.

Finally, *house* is used in a broad sense to signify domain; the rule or influence of a person or thing, such as the house of bondage (Exod. 13:3), house of rebellion (Ezek. 3:9), or house of mourning (Jer. 16:5).

THE HOUSE OF GOD

One of the most significant biblical uses of the word *house* is in reference to the "house of God." Jesus taught that this house belongs to his Father (John 14:2).

As before, *house* used in this context can have more than one meaning. It can refer to a literal place where the Father dwells: either the tent of meeting, the tabernacle, the temple, or heaven. It can refer to the Father's family line: his children who are the church of God. Or finally, it can be used in a figurative sense to refer to the Father's domain, his place of rule and influence.

Often biblical references to the house of God have multiple meanings referring to both a literal and figurative place at the same time. We cannot always define exactly what or where this place is; however, we do know that the house of God is any place where the glory of the Father dwells. It is *any place where God makes his home.*

David expressed this exact idea in Psalm 26:8: "I love the house where you live, O LORD, the place where your glory dwells" (NIV).

WHAT IS THE FATHER'S HOUSE LIKE?

If you wanted to buy a house, you would want to look at it to check out its physical properties. You would want to see the number and size of the bedrooms, how large the kitchen is, whether the house has a fireplace, and where the laundry room is located.

The apostle John prophetically described some of the physical characteristics of the Father's house in the book of Revelation (most notably in chapters 4, 20, and 21). But most often, when the Bible talks about the Father's house, it speaks of characteristics other than the physical.

The following list describes what the Father's house is like:
- It is the place where the Father is on the throne.
  (Ps. 132:13–14)
- It is the Father's resting place. (Ps. 66:1–2)
- It is a place of splendor and majesty. (1 Chron. 16:27)
- It is adorned with holiness. (Ps. 93:5)
- It is a place of glory. (Hag. 2:6–9)
- It is full of goodness. (Ps. 65:4)
- It is a place of worship. (Ps. 132:7)
- It is a place of prayer. (Isa. 56:7)
- It is a place of thanksgiving. (Ps. 116:17–19)
- It is a place of fellowship. (Ps. 55:14)
- It includes people from all nations. (Isa. 56:7)
- It includes people from all social standings. (Ps. 36:7–9)

- It is a place of singing. (Ps. 135:2–3)
- It is a place of learning. (Isa. 2:2–3)
- It is a place of safety. (Ps. 27:5)
- It is a place of strength and joy. (1 Chron. 16:27)

Though astonishingly beautiful, the thing that makes the Father's house so attractive is not its physical appearance. Its real beauty is found in him. All else pales in significance. What makes the Father's house so amazing is, quite simply, that it is his. It is the place where he lives. His house is beautiful because he is there.

THE FATHER'S CHILDREN FLOURISH IN HIS HOUSE

For the past year my husband and I have been discussing the merits of moving from our suburban house to a house in the country. The primary consideration, and the focus of our discussion, is whether the move would be beneficial for our children. We want to live in a place where our children will flourish.

The Father's house is the place where his children flourish. Read the following passages from the Psalms and notice all the phrases that indicate how a child of God flourishes in the Father's house.

They feast on the abundance of your house;
you give them drink from your river of delights.
For with you is the fountain of life;
in your light we see light. (Ps. 36:8–9 NIV)

The righteous will flourish like a palm tree,
they will grow like a cedar of Lebanon;
planted in the house of the LORD,
they will flourish in the courts of our God.
They will still bear fruit in old age,
they will stay fresh and green,
proclaiming, "The LORD is upright;
he is my Rock, and there is no wickedness in him."
(Ps. 92:12–15 NIV)

But I am like an olive tree
flourishing in the house of God;
I trust in God's unfailing love
for ever and ever. (Ps. 52:8 NIV)

I love that word *flourish!* To flourish means "to thrive, to be vigorous or in good health, to reach the height of development." Children of God flourish in their father's house. David uses the analogy of a palm, a cedar, and an olive tree. That leads me to consider the plants in my mother's house. My mom has an incredibly green thumb. She has dozens and dozens of plants in her home, all of which she dotes on and pampers on an ongoing basis. The net result is that her plants are healthy and vigorous. They grow large and bloom profusely.

David says that when we are securely planted in the house of our Father God, we flourish like palms, cedars, and olives. The tree symbolism is significant. The palm is an emblem of victory or triumph. The tall, stately cedar is noted for its durability and fragrance. The olive is called the "king of the trees" (Judg. 9:8). If undisturbed, it can grow for centuries. It is both durable and fruitful. Its branch is a symbol of peace and friendship, while its fruit is a most valuable source of oil.

The Father leads his children to his house. He plants them in his court so they can send their roots down deep, be established, and flourish. "In your unfailing love you will lead the people you have redeemed. In your strength you will guide them to your holy dwelling. . . . You will bring them in and plant them on the mountain of your inheritance—the place, O LORD, you made for your dwelling, the sanctuary, O Lord, your hands established" (Exod. 15:13, 17 NIV).

I find the thought of finding a place where I can thrive, flourish, and stay "fresh and green" very compelling, don't you? Health, wholeness, abundance, and delight are what most people spend their lives searching for. Just think, this is what you can experience in the Father's house!

Now and Not Yet

The promise of being with our Father is the thought that draws and motivates every child that is his. It is the deepest desire of the Christian heart. It is the groaning, the longing, the hope, the crown, and the reason for our endurance. It is the Abba cry that will not be completely satisfied until we see him face-to-face and he wipes every tear and every disappointment from our eyes. Revelation 21 is my favorite passage of the Bible. I am moved to tears every time I read it, for the passage speaks of the time when all of my hopes and longings will be fulfilled, the time when I will finally see my loving Father face-to-face:

> And I heard a loud voice from heaven saying, "Behold, the tabernacle of God is with men, and He will dwell with them, and they shall be His people. God Himself will be with them and be their God. And God will wipe away every tear from their eyes; there shall be no more death, nor sorrow, nor crying. There shall be no more pain, for the former things have passed away."

> . . . And He said to me, . . . "I will give of the fountain of the water of life freely to him who thirsts. He who overcomes shall inherit all things, and I will be his God and he shall be My son." (Rev. 21:3–4, 6–7)

The Father's house is in the heart of every individual believer (Ps. 66:1–2; Heb. 3:4–6). It is also in the church, the body of believers, who are built upon the precious cornerstone of Jesus Christ (1 Pet. 2:5). And it is in heaven, his eternal dwelling place (John 14:1–3).

One day we will see him face-to-face in his house in heaven. But even now, we are able to enter in by drawing near in our hearts. The Father's house is beautiful. It is your dream home. It is everything you could ever desire, everything you could ever hope for, and even more. The Father bids you to enter and enjoy.

Do you feel dry, lifeless, and defeated in your spirit? Let me tell you what your problem is. You are homesick. You are yearning for that place where you will flourish. Your heart is longing for the Father's house. Even now you can enter in. Why don't you take a moment to pray to the Father and express that childlike desire, "I want to go home!"

CHAPTER 28

THE JOY OF HIS HOUSE

If there lurks in most modern minds the notion that to desire our own good and earnestly to hope for the enjoyment of it is a bad thing, I submit that this notion has crept in from Kant and the Stoics and is no part of the Christian faith. Indeed, if we consider the unblushing promises of reward and the staggering nature of the rewards promised in the Gospels, it would seem that our Lord finds our desires, not too strong, but too weak. We are half-hearted creatures, fooling about with drink and sex and ambition when infinite joy is offered us, like an ignorant child who wants to go on making mud pies in a slum because he cannot imagine what is meant by the offer of a holiday at the sea. We are far too easily pleased.

—C. S. Lewis[1]

Now to Him who is able to keep you from stumbling,
And to present you faultless
Before the presence of His glory with exceeding joy.
(Jude 24)

Oh, send out Your light and Your truth!
Let them lead me;
Let them bring me to Your holy hill
And to Your tabernacle.
Then I will go the altar of God,
To God my exceeding joy;
And on the harp I will praise You,
O God, my God. (Ps. 43:3–4)

You will show me the path of life;
In Your presence is fullness of joy;
At Your right hand are pleasures forevermore. (Ps. 16:11)

For further study, read about the example of Moses, who gave up the happiness of Pharaoh's court for the greater riches of the Father's house (Heb. 11:23–27).

All men seek happiness. This is without exception.

—BLAISE PASCAL

Happiness is no laughing matter. It is the serious business of humanity.

—JAMES HOUSTON

Everyone wants to be happy. The desire to be happy is a powerful, if not *the* most powerful, motivating factor in human existence. Think about it for a moment. Is not the reason we work, and eat, and acquire things, and make friends, and love, our own happiness? The one who gives is just as motivated by the promise of happiness as the one who hoards. The latter seeks happiness in gathering things for self, while the former seeks it in securing good things for others.

Those who are perpetually miserable also seek happiness. Perhaps they think that in their misery and criticism they might correct the world, or set themselves above it, and thus be happy. Even a person committing suicide seeks his own happiness. Not being able to bear the pain of being miserable, he seeks to end his misery by ending his life.

Humans are, by nature, pleasure seekers. This fact causes some Christians to shudder in disgust and seek to put aside this fleshly vice. In some twisted way they begin to regard misery as virtue. However, the Bible's solution to pleasure seeking, far from condemning it, is to commend it toward that which brings the most pleasure. Children of God are told—in fact, they are commanded!—to seek the highest pleasure possible: "Delight yourself also in the LORD, and He shall give you the desires of your heart" (Ps. 37:4).

The problem with pleasure, as C. S. Lewis pointed out, is not that we aim for it, but that in aiming, we aim too low. Our desire is far too weak. We are "half-hearted creatures," settling for what brings us a fleeting measure of happiness instead of pursuing that which brings us abundant and eternal happiness.

The premise of this chapter is that we have a happy God who lives in a happy house and who wants happy children. Perhaps the definitions of *happiness* and *joy* will help you unpack this thought. *Happy* means "delight, being pleased, having a glad feeling." *Joy* refers to "excitement or pleasurable feeling caused by the acquisition or expectation of good; the cause of satisfaction and happiness."

Did you notice a difference? Happiness describes a feeling. It is not associated with a value, good or bad. A person can feel happy regardless of the value of what caused her to feel that way. One person feels happy through illicit sex, pornography, cheating, lying, and another through charity, giving, and honesty.

Joy, on the other hand, is the feeling that is caused by expecting or acquiring something good. It is anchored to the value of that which is received. And it is the cause of happiness. Happy says, "I feel good." Joy says, "The value of what is happening here (or what I expect to happen as a result) is good, so I feel good." Therefore, joy can produce happiness in even the most miserable circumstance.

Being joyful is not the same as being happy, but it does include it. A person can feel happy without ever having joy. But the person who is joyful will most surely feel happy as well.

Joy breeds happiness. Thus, Christians can be just as reckless in seeking happiness as their non-Christian counterparts. The crucial difference, however, is that Christians have been redeemed and renewed by the power of God. A renewed mind views happiness through a larger lens. It has an eye toward the quality and duration of its happiness. It sees that a joyful happiness, grounded in goodness, is great and lasting. A happiness divorced from goodness is so fleeting and deceptive that in comparison it is not happiness at all. The renewed mind knows that we find happiness of the deepest kind where we find the deepest good. And the renewed mind knows that the deepest good is found in God.

A HAPPY GOD

God is a happy being. The Father has joy in his glory (Isa. 42:8), joy in his Son (Isa. 42:1), joy in his creation (Gen. 1:31), joy in his children (Zeph. 3:17), joy in giving them good things (Jer. 32:40–41), and joy in his redemptive plan. Jesus is happy, just like his Father (John 17:13). And the Holy Spirit is happy too (Rom. 14:18).

Think about the paragraph you just read and ask yourself a question. How do you "see" Father God? When you think of the mighty Creator of the universe, do you see him with a smile or a scowl?

Jude 24 refers to God as the one "who is able to keep you from falling and to present you before his glorious presence without fault and with great joy" (NIV). At the prospect of having us presented faultless in his presence, the Father's heart is filled with joy.

Somewhere I remember learning a simple chorus based on Nehemiah 8:10. Nehemiah declared: "Go and enjoy choice food and sweet drinks, and send some to those who have nothing prepared. This day is sacred to our Lord. Do not grieve, for the joy of the LORD is your strength" (NIV). The chorus simply repeats, "The joy of the Lord is our strength." What energy we can receive from learning to celebrate and rest in the joy of our Father God.

JOY IN HIS HOUSE

The Father's house is a joyful place. King David confirmed that there is "strength and joy in his dwelling place" (1 Chron. 16:27 NIV). He said that "fullness of joy" and "pleasures forevermore" could be found there (Ps. 16:11). Joy and gladness are found in the house of God, as well as thanksgiving and the voice of melody (Isa. 51:3). In this house the river of delight runs deep for all who want to drink (Ps. 36:8–9).

Psalm 65:4 says, "Blessed are those you choose and bring near to live in your courts! We are filled with the good things of your house, of your holy temple" (NIV). The term *blessed*, when used of humans, means "happy." One Hebrew dictionary describes this blessedness as a heightened state of happiness and joy, implying favorable circumstances, often resulting from the kind acts of God.

The house of the Father is a happy place. The people who drink from his river of delight are happy people. Every time the doors open and another soul enters, great joy and happiness erupt. The angels and all the saints make a fuss and ruckus that would make the most satisfying party on earth look like a dirge. No wonder David exclaimed with delight: "I love the house where you live" (Ps. 26:8 NIV).

THE FATHER WANTS HAPPY CHILDREN

Does it surprise you that the Father wants his children to be happy? Perhaps you were thinking that happiness for Christians is reserved for heaven: Misery now means happiness then. If so, you are wrong.

Jesus expected that his own joy would remain with his disciples: "These things I have spoken to you, that My joy may remain in you, and that your joy may be full" (John 15:11).

He told them, "Your heart will rejoice, and your joy no one will take from you" (John 16:22). In the following verse, note the phrase that describes the type of joy you can have even before you get to heaven:

> Though now you do not see Him, yet believing, you rejoice
> with joy inexpressible and full of glory, receiving the end of
> your faith—the salvation of your souls. (1 Pet. 1:8–9)

How happy are you? Do you feel that you have "joy inexpressible and full of glory"? How much joy do you have in your life? However you respond, I have a word for you. Your Father wants the answer to be more.

COSTLY JOY

Don't get me wrong. The Father wants his children to be overflowing with happy joy, but that doesn't mean that he guarantees us lives free from pain. Joy costs—sometimes dearly. For the joy that was set before him, Jesus humbled himself, took on the nature of a servant, endured mocking, misunderstanding, and even the shame of the cross (Heb. 2:12). Joy cost Jesus his life. It cost the Father his Son. Joy does not come cheaply.

The early believers knew full well the cost of joy. James counted it all joy when he fell into various trials (James 1:2). Paul said that it was in the midst of a great trial of affliction that the abundance of the Macedonian's joy abounded (2 Cor. 8:2). The early believers found joy in affliction (1 Thess. 1:6), in chains and tribulations (Acts 20:23–24), in weaknesses, insults, hardships, persecutions, and difficulties (2 Cor. 12:10).

The following passage describes some things Paul experienced. Carefully compare every negative thing and every positive he identifies.

> Rather, as servants of God we commend ourselves in every way: in great endurance; in troubles, hardships and distresses; in beatings, imprisonments and riots; in hard work, sleepless nights and hunger; in purity, understanding, patience and kindness; in the Holy Spirit and in sincere love; in truthful speech and in the power of God; with weapons of righteousness in the right hand and in the left; through glory and dishonor, bad report and good report; genuine, yet regarded as impostors; known, yet regarded as unknown; dying, and yet we live on; beaten, and yet not killed; sorrowful, yet always rejoicing; poor, yet making many rich; having nothing, and yet possessing everything. (2 Cor. 6:4–10 NIV)

Paul said, "If I am being poured out as a drink offering on the sacrifice and service of your faith, I am glad and rejoice" (Phil. 2:17–18). He also said, "For I consider that the sufferings of this present time are not worthy to be compared with the glory which shall be revealed in us. . . . In all these things we are more than conquerors through Him who loved us" (Rom. 8:18, 37).

In light of Paul's words, I wonder how he would have answered the above question. Do you think he would have regarded anything in the list as being negative? Or would he have considered every situation he experienced as positive?

Paul was a happy man. His was a deep, serious, costly sort of happiness that was caused by the joy of pursuing the highest good. Paul was happy because his eye remained focused on the day when "the ransomed of the LORD shall return, and come to Zion with singing, with everlasting joy on their heads. They shall obtain joy and gladness; Sorrow and sighing shall flee away" (Isa. 51:11).

What about you? Do you believe that the Father is a happy God who lives in a happy house and who wants you to be happy? Are you like the man who unearthed a great treasure hidden in a field, and who, in his joy, went and sold everything he had to buy that field (Matt. 13:44)? Ask the Father to show you more of the priceless treasure of his house so that you, with joy, may be willing to pay any price to enter in.

CHAPTER 29

MAKING YOUR HOME
WITH THE FATHER

Your home is familiar to you. No one has to tell you how to locate your bedroom; you don't need directions to the kitchen. After a hard day scrambling to find your way around in the world, it's assuring to come home to a place you know. God can be equally familiar to you. With time you can learn where to go for nourishment, where to hide for protection, where to turn for guidance. Just as your earthly house is a place of refuge, so God's house is a place of peace. God's house has never been plundered, his walls have never been breached.

God can be your dwelling place.

God wants to be your dwelling place. He has no interest in being a weekend getaway or a Sunday bungalow or a summer cottage. Don't consider using God as a vacation cabin or an eventual retirement home. He wants you under his roof now and always. He wants to be your mailing address, your point of reference; he wants to be your home.

—Max Lucado[1]

As for me, I will see Your face in righteousness; I shall be satisfied when I awake in Your likeness. (Ps. 17:15)

Jesus answered and said to him, "If anyone loves Me, he will keep My word; and My Father will love him, and We will come to him and make Our home with him." (John 14:23)

Thou has formed us for Thyself, and our hearts are restless till they find rest in Thee.

—AUGUSTINE

In the second book of C. S. Lewis's Space Trilogy, a man named Ransom is sent to a planet called Perelandra. Perelandra is a new planet, innocent in the perfection of its creation. Perelandra's only visible inhabitant, the queen, is yet unblemished by doubt, temptation, and sin.

On Perelandra, Ransom wanders into some woods where great globes of yellow fruit hang from the trees. Picking one, he pokes his thumb through the smooth, firm rind and drinks of the exquisite nectar. The taste is pleasure beyond his experience. On Earth, wars would be fought and friends betrayed for just one draught. He lets the empty gourd fall and instinctively reaches to pluck another one. But as his hand nears the fruit, he stops.

For whatever reason, it appears to him better not to taste again. On Earth, pleasure begs repetition. But on Perelandra, the experience of drinking the nectar is so satisfying and complete that repeating it would seem vulgar. Just one is enough.

Have you ever noticed how all satisfaction in this life is laced with longing? You eat a plump, sweet strawberry and right away reach for another. The desired easy chair is bought, but your eyes soon turn toward the space that needs a table. Your daughter has come to visit, but within a few days of returning to college, you long to see her again.

Can you imagine a young woman telling her newlywed husband, the delight of her heart, "Thank you. I am satisfied and have had enough of you now. You can go away." Of course not. The greater the satisfaction, the greater the longing.

CHILDREN OF THE BURNING HEART

All satisfaction in this life is still shot through with longing and all genuine longing has tasted the satisfying water of life.

—JOHN PIPER[2]

Come near any godly person, and you will soon feel the heat of their passion for knowing God. This passion motivates their prayers, fastings, meditations, sacrifice, service, and all self-discipline and self-denial. So intense is this desire that their happiness and even their will to exist hinge on it. And the times when they do taste and see him, the satisfaction is all the sweeter for the struggle.

All great Christian heroes of the past have walked this path: King David, whose soul panted for God as the deer for water (Ps. 42:1–2); the apostle Paul, who "pressed on" to take hold of him; the martyrs, who died so as not to deny; Teresa of Avila who was impassioned with constant longing; A. W. Tozer who said, "To have found God and still to pursue Him is the soul's paradox of love, scorned indeed by the too-easily-satisfied religionist, but justified in happy experience by the children of the burning heart."[3]

The Psalms are filled with the desperate desire of the seeker and the exuberant satisfaction of the finder. In the following verses from the Psalms, savor all the phrases that indicate the object of David's desire and satisfaction:

> How lovely is your dwelling place,
> O Lord Almighty!
> My soul yearns, even faints,
> for the courts of the Lord;
> my heart and my flesh cry out
> for the living God. (Ps. 84:1–2 NIV)

> Whom have I in heaven but You?
> And there is none upon earth that I desire besides You.
> (Ps. 73:25)

> As for me, I will see Your face in righteousness;
> I shall be satisfied when I awake in Your likeness.
> (Ps. 17:15)

> We shall be satisfied with the goodness of Your house,
> Of Your holy temple. (Ps. 65:4)

> O God, You are my God;
> Early will I seek You;
> My soul thirsts for You;

My flesh longs for You
In a dry and thirsty land
Where there is no water.
So I have looked for You in the sanctuary,
To see Your power and Your glory. . . .
My soul shall be satisfied as with marrow and fatness,
And my mouth shall praise You with joyful lips.
(Ps. 63:1–2, 5)

Based on these verses, we have no doubt who the object of David's desire and the source of his satisfaction is, do we? David sought God not out of some religious obligation but from a deep love grounded in joy.

The one who desires God and dwells in the satisfaction of the Father's house partakes in the paradox of love. As she enjoys her Father, her desire of him becomes more insatiable and her thirsting more unquenchable. She becomes, as Tozer described it, a "Child of the Burning Heart."

Making Your Home with the Father

If you are a Christian, you have entered into the Father's house. But do you feel as though the Father's house is your home? Jesus promised that he and the Father would make their home with all who follow him (John 15:23). The Father is not content that you stay in the foyer of salvation but wants you to take Jesus' hand and explore all the rooms.

Enter the massive kitchen, where the aroma of fresh-baked bread fills the air, and a feast of abundance awaits you. The study is filled with books of knowledge and the history of God's people as found in the Word. Entering through the doors you immediately feel an increase in your desire to know more about your Father. Here you may sit in the comfortable big chair, read, and learn. Just off the study is the sunroom, a place for solitude and meditation.

In a quiet wing of the house, bedrooms provide rest for the weary. Blankets of peace soothe each agitation so the saints can sleep. The bathroom contains the cleansing showers of repentance. Did you notice the sweet fragrance? And the clean radiance of all who exit this room? Next to the bathroom you will find the laundry room, where old clothes may be traded for new.

As you walk down the hall, you will begin to hear the laughter and noise of the family room. The diversity in this room is astonishing. A veiled Moroccan is teaching a Swede how to spin silk. A group of theologians are discussing dispensationalism. A biker from San Francisco is letting a Russian soldier try on his leather jacket. A royal princess plays chess with a former convict. In the corner, musicians form an ad hoc worship band with accordion, zither, bagpipe, violin, fife, timpani, and electric guitar. The room bursts with the sounds and colors of all nations. It is a place of love and acceptance.

Just outside of the family room is the workshop and toolshed. The keeper of the shed will give you the necessary tools—gifts of the Holy Spirit—to equip you for the work the Father wants you to do.

Follow your Brother, if you will, to the furnace room. As you walk through the halls, take note of the absence of closets. In the house of God, nothing is hidden. Open the door of the furnace room and feel the heat of the burning fuel of prayer. The power panel is located beside the furnace. Observe how the whole house is wired with the power of the Spirit of God.

And now Jesus will lead you to the great room, into the presence of his Father. You feel awed, even nervous, as you walk in. This room is more splendid than any king's castle and cozier than the quaintest cottage, but you hardly notice. What you notice is him. "Most Holy, Almighty God!" you stammer, as you fall down on your face.

He comes and crouches before you, gently raising your chin so that you are gazing directly into his eyes. "Call me 'Father,'" he says with a smile. "I am glad you have come. I have been waiting."

Walk with your Father and Brother out of the great room into the garden of worship. Revel in the beauty. Bask in his presence. Be awed. Be serious. Be satisfied. Dance, sing, and rejoice! Drink from his river of delight. The river is deep, as is the garden. This is the place where you are able to gaze at the beauty of God free from all distraction. Once you have been in the garden, you will want to stay forever.

However, whether you are able to enter the garden, how long you stay, and how far into it you can go depends not on your own will but on how familiar and comfortable you are in all the other rooms of the Father's house. Those who are unfamiliar with the rooms of the word, repentance, or prayer, for example, will not be able to move far into the garden of worship. Thus, for the satisfaction of seeing the Father in the garden, it is necessary constantly to move about, seeking to become familiar with all the details, manners, and way of his great house.

Enter in. Press farther. Become a child of the burning heart whose longing is for the Father and who is only satisfied dwelling in his house, near to the Father's heart.

David said, "Surely goodness and mercy shall follow me all the days of my life; and I will dwell in the house of the LORD forever" (Ps. 23:6).

A FINAL ASSIGNMENT

Remember the Father's Day card you made for your heavenly Father at the end of part 1 of our journey together? Retrieve it from the place you put it. Based on what God has shown you as you have studied his Word through these pages, is there anything in the card that you would change? Have you matured in your understanding of what the Father is like?

Take some time to write a letter to your heavenly Father based on what you now see. In the note, thank him for the truth he has revealed to you through this study. If possible, identify ways your perception of him has changed. Tell him you would like your relationship with him to continue to grow. Write whatever is on your heart. When you are finished, you may want to fasten the card inside the front cover of this book and the letter inside the back cover.

You have come to almost the end of this book, but your relationship with your heavenly Father will go on. Whether that relationship is young and fresh or long established, God has so much more for you and for me. I am excited to think that I've hardly even begun to explore the wonders of my Father's house. I don't want anything to keep me from fully exploring every nook and cranny. And I wish the same for you. Oh, how I long for you to grow in the joy of the Father's house until that time when we meet and get to explore it together.

CHAPTER 30

KNOWING HIM BY NAME

"Yes, Lord, . . . we wait for you; your name
and renown are the desire of our hearts."

—ISAIAH 26:8 (NIV)

I'm so glad that you joined me for this journey into the Father's house! I hope that through these pages you've come to know him at a deeper, more intimate level and that your love for him has grown. What's amazing is that we've only just skimmed the surface of this vast treasure. There are countless more riches to discover and so many more rooms to explore! In this last chapter I'd like to crack open a few more doors into Father God's character by introducing you to his many names. I hope this glimpse will whet your appetite to continue pressing ever closer to his heart and ever deeper into the wonders of his house.

Shakespeare once said, "What's in a name? That which we call a rose by any other name would smell as sweet." Solomon disagreed. He said that a good name is better than precious ointment and that it ought to be preferred over great riches (Eccl. 7:1; Prov. 22:1). To be fair, Shakespeare was thinking of a name merely as a label, while Solomon was referring more to a person's reputation. But consider this: would a rose be as popular a symbol of love if it was called "stinkweed" or "death thorn"?

Names are important. They are identifying marks that distinguish us from others. Remember that powerful scene in the movie *Gladiator* when the hero reveals his name? As a gladiator slave, he had been known to his master and comrades only as "the Spaniard." But when the emperor forced him to take off his iron mask and make himself known, he boldly declared, "My name is Maximus Decimus Meridius; commander of the Armies of the North; general of the Felix Legions; loyal servant to the true emperor, Marcus Aurelius; father to a murdered son; husband to a murdered wife . . . and I will have my vengeance, in this life or in the next."

The gladiator's name was his identity. It defined his character as well as his relationships and his purpose. Names are highly important. We can't really know a person until we know his or her name. In the world of truckers, a driver's identity on the citizen's band radio (CB) is referred to as a "handle." A handle, like a name, allows us to get a grip on the person with whom we are interacting. It's the same way with Father God. In getting to know him by name, we can get a better grip on his personality and come to know and love him better.

My great-grandfather had a long name: Albin Albert Christian Christoph Gottlieb Max Thomas. Each name meant something. He was named after a plethora of friends and relatives whom, for whatever reason, his father wanted to honor. The tradition was passed down from generation to generation. Thankfully, in naming me, my father decided that he would honor only my grandmothers, Marie and Anna, and I therefore have only two names, as compared to my great-grandfather's seven.

The Bible reveals that Father God has dozens of names. Each name means something. God's different names show us different aspects of his nature, or different ways he relates to us. Knowing his names thus enables us to know him better. Of all the names of God, there are three that are the most prominent: *Elohim*, *Yahweh*, and *Adonai*.

ELOHIM, ALL-POWERFUL CREATOR

The first verse in Scripture refers to Father God as Elohim: "In the beginning Elohim created the heavens and the earth." This name for God appears more than thirty times in the first chapter of Genesis alone. The Hebrew word Elohim is from *El*, meaning "the strong One or the Creator," and *alah*, "to swear or bind oneself with an oath, which implies faithfulness." The name *Elohim* reveals the incomparably great power, strength, creativity, and eternal faithfulness of our Father.

When God spoke to Moses from the burning bush in Exodus 3:14, Moses requested to know God's name. And God said to Moses, "I AM WHO I AM." He said, "Thus you shall say to the children of Israel, 'I AM has sent me to you.'"

In Hebrew, the name "I AM" is *Yahweh*. Jewish scribes wrote it with only the four consonants YHWH and no vowels. The Jews regarded the name as so holy that they refrained from spelling it in its entirety and refused to speak it out loud. Instead, they referred to it as "the name," "the extraordinary name," or "the distinguished name." Historically, this name was spoken only by the priests in the temple when blessing the people (Num. 6:23–27). The high priest also spoke it annually on Yom Kippur, the Day of Atonement, so that its pronunciation would not be lost.

The name YHWH occurs almost seven thousand times in the Bible. When a Jewish scribe copying the Scriptures came to the sacred name, he would set aside his quill and get a new one with which to write it. Then, he would break and discard the quill so that no other word would ever flow from it. In the King James Version of the Bible, the name YHWH is honored by writing its translations in capital and small capital letters: LORD.

What then is the meaning or significance of this name of our Father? The root word of Yahweh is *hayah,* which means "to be or become." Therefore, the name is linked to the concept of life and being. To be is to live. Thus, the name indicates that God is the one who in himself possesses life and permanent existence. Apart from him nothing exists, and without him there is no life. Our Father God is life and he gives life. Therefore, he is the only one in whom we can truly experience life as it was meant to be.

Adonai, Our Master

The third primary name for God is Adonai. *Adon* refers to the master of a slave. The name is positional. It indicates who has headship or authority in a relationship. The name *Adonai* is also translated in our Bibles by the word "Lord." But in this instance only the first letter is capitalized. This name of God occurs about three hundred times in the Old Testament. The use of *Adonai* illustrates the proper relationship between Father God and his children. It indicates that God is the rightful master of every member of the human family. He is the cosmic Father, the head of all humanity. Therefore, it is proper and right that we give him the utmost respect, honor, and obedience.

GOD'S GLORIOUS NAMES

Father God's names range from the great and incomprehensible name, "Yahweh El Elyon—the Lord, the Most High God," to the personal and intimate name, "Abba Daddy." He has dozens of names. Each one provides insight into his character and the nature of his relationship with us. To close this chapter and this book, I have provided a list of the names of Father God. Take some time to meditate on each one. If you can't commit the time to do this right now, why don't you set aside some time to work your way through it over the next few days? As you are meditating, try to identify which of his names mean the most to you and which of his names indicate an aspect of his character and/or nature that you would like to know more of. See if you can join with Isaiah, who prayed, "Yes, LORD, . . . we wait for you; your name and renown are the desire of our hearts" (Isa. 26:8 NIV).

> *Yahweh El Elohim*, the LORD God of Gods (Josh. 22:22)
> *Yahweh Elohim*, the LORD God (Gen. 2:4)
> *Yahweh Elohe Abothekem*, the LORD God of Your Fathers (Josh. 18:3)
> *Yahweh El Elyon*, the LORD, the Most High God (Gen. 14:22)
> *Yahweh El Emeth*, the LORD God of Truth (Ps. 31:5)
> *Yahweh El Gemuwal*, the LORD God of Recompenses (Jer. 51:56)
> *Yahweh Elohim Tsebaoth*, the LORD God of Hosts (Ps. 59:5)
> *Yahweh Elohe Yeshuathi*, the LORD God of My Salvation (Ps. 88:1)
> *Yahweh Elohe Yisrael*, the LORD God of Israel (Ps. 41:13)
> *Elohim*, God (Gen. 1:1)
> *Elohim Bashamayim*, God in Heaven (Josh. 2:11)
> *El Bethel*, God of the House of God (Gen. 35:7)
> *Elohe Chaseddi*, the God of My Mercy (Ps. 59:10)
> *El Elyon*, the Most High God (Gen. 14:18)
> *El Emunah*, the Faithful God (Deut. 7:9)

El Gibbor, Mighty God (Isa. 9:6)

El Hakabodh, The God of Glory (Ps. 29:3)

El Hay, the Living God (Josh. 3:10)

El Hayyay, God of My Life (Ps. 42:8)

Elohim Kedoshim, Holy God (Josh. 24:19)

El Kanna, Jealous God (Exod. 20:5)

Elohe Mauzi, God of My Strength (Ps. 43:2)

Elohim Machase Lanu, God Our Refuge (Ps. 62:8)

Eli Malekhi, God My King (Ps. 68:24)

El Marom, God Most High (Mic. 6:6)

El Nekamouth, God That Avengeth (Ps. 18:47)

El Nose, God That Forgave (Ps. 99:8)

Elohenu Olam, Our Everlasting God (Ps. 48:14)

Elohim Ozer Li, God My Helper (Ps. 54:4)

El Rai, God Sees Me (Gen. 16:13)

El Sali, God, My Rock (Ps. 42:9)

El Shaddai, Almighty God (Gen. 17:1–2)

Elohim Sophtim Ga-arets, God That Judges in the Earth
      (Ps. 58:11)

El Simchath Gili, God My Exceeding Joy (Ps. 43:4)

Elohim Tsebaoth, God of Hosts (Ps. 80:7)

Elohe Tishuathi, God of My Salvation (Ps. 18:46; 51:14)

Elohe Tadeki, God My Righteousness (Ps. 4:1)

Elohe Yakob, God of Israel (Ps. 20:1)

Yahweh, the LORD (Exod. 6:2–3)

Adonai Yahweh, LORD God (Gen. 15:2)

Yahweh Adon Kol Ha-arets, the LORD, the Lord of All the Earth
      (Josh. 3:11)

Yawey Bore, the LORD Creator (Isa. 40:28)

Yahweh Chereb, the LORD, the Sword (Deut. 33:29)

Yahweh Eli, the LORD My God (Ps. 18:2)

Yawey Elyon, the LORD Most High (Gen. 14:18–20)

Yahweh Gibbor Milchamah, the LORD Our Defense (Ps. 89:18)

Yahweh Goelekh, the LORD Your Redeemer (Isa. 49:26)

Yahweh Hashopet, the LORD the Judge (Judg. 11:27)

Yahweh Hoshiah, O LORD Save (Ps. 20:9)

Yahweh Immeka, the LORD Is with You (Judg. 6:12)

Yahweh Izuz Wegibbor, the LORD Strong and Mighty (Ps. 24:8)

Yahweh-Jireh, the LORD Shall Provide (Gen. 22:14)
Yahweh Kabodhi, the LORD My Glory (Ps. 3:3)
Yahweh Kanna Shemo, the LORD Whose Name Is Jealous
    (Exod. 34:14)
Yahweh Keren-Yishi, the LORD the Horn of My Salvation
    (Ps. 18:2)
Yahweh Machsi, the LORD My Refuge (Ps. 91:9)
Yahweh Magen, the LORD, the Shield (Deut. 33:29)
Yahweh Mauzzam, the LORD Their Strength (Ps. 37:39)
Ha-melech Yahweh, the LORD the King (Ps. 98:6)
Yahweh Melch Olam, the LORD King Forever (Ps. 10:16)
Yahweh Mephalti, the LORD My Deliverer (Ps. 18:2)
Yahweh Mekaddishkhem, the LORD That Sanctifies You
    (Exod. 31:13)
Yahweh Metsudhathi, the LORD My Fortress (Ps. 8:2)
Yahweh Mishgabbit, the LORD My High Tower (Ps. 18:2)
Yahweh Moshiekh, the LORD Your Savior (Isa. 49:26)
Yahweh-Nissi, the LORD My Banner (Exod. 17:15)
Yahweh Ori, the LORD My Light (Ps. 27:1)
Yahweh Uzzi, the LORD My Strength (Ps. 28:7)
Yahweh Rophe, the LORD Our Healer (Exod. 15:26)
Yahweh Roi, the LORD My Shepherd (Ps. 23:1)
Yahweh Sabaoth, the LORD of Hosts (1 Sam. 1:2)
Yahweh Sali, the LORD My Rock (Ps. 18:2)
Yahweh Shalom, the LORD Our Peace (Judg. 6:24)
Light (Ps. 27:1)
Dwelling Place (Ps. 90:1)
Fortress (Ps. 91:2)
Stronghold (Ps. 18:2)
Tower of Strength (Ps. 61:3)
Refuge (Ps. 46:1)
Shield (Ps. 18:30)
Hiding Place (Ps. 32:7)
Rock (Hab. 1:12)
Strength (Ps. 46:1)
My Portion (Ps. 142:5)
My Cup (Ps. 16:5)
Beautiful Crown and Glorious Diadem (Isa. 28:5)

Potter (Isa. 64:8)

Husband or Lord (Isa. 54:5; Jer. 31:32)

Loving-kindness (Ps. 144:2)

King of Glory (Ps. 24:7)

King of Israel (Zeph. 3:15)

Lord of All the Earth (Mic. 4:13)

Ancient of Days (Dan. 7:9)

Incomparable God (Exod. 9:14; Deut. 33:26; 2 Sam. 7:22; Isa. 46:5, 9; Jer. 10:6)

The God of Our Fathers [*Elohay Avotaynu*] (Acts 7:32)

God of All Comfort [*Elohay Kol HaNechamah*] (2 Cor. 1:3)

God of Peace [*Elohay Shalom*] (Heb. 13:20)

The God of Glory [*Elohay Kavod*] (Acts 7:2)

The Living God [*Elohay Chaiyim*] (2 Cor. 3:3; 6:16)

The God of Israel [*Elohay Yisrael*] (Matt. 15:31)

LORD Almighty [*Yahweh Shaddai*] (2 Cor. 6:18)

The Almighty [*Shaddai*] (Rev. 1:8)

Power [*Ha Gevurah*] (Mark 14:62)

The Creator [*HaBoray*] (Rom. 1:25; 1 Pet. 4:19)

The Most High God [*El Elyon*] (Heb. 7:1)

The Divine Nature (Rom. 1:20; 2 Pet. 1:4)

Lord of Armies: [*Yahweh Tz'vaot*] (James 5:4)

The Majestic Glory (2 Pet. 1:17)

The Majesty (Heb. 1:3)

The King of the Nations (Rev. 15:3)

The Lawgiver and Judge (James 4:12)

The Eternal Immortal Invisible King (1 Tim. 1:17)

Sovereign (1 Tim. 6:15)

Heaven (Matt. 21:25)

Consuming Fire (Heb. 12:29)

God the Father (2 Tim. 1:2)

Father of Our Lord Yeshua, the Messiah (Col. 1:3)

The Father of Lights (James 1:17)

The Father of Glory (Eph. 1:17)

The Father of Spirits (Heb. 12:9)

Father of Mercies (2 Cor. 1:3)

Our Father (Matt. 6:9)

Abba [Daddy] (Rom. 8:15)

Our Father God is wonderful beyond words. He loves you dearly and longs for you to press ever nearer to his heart. He wants you to come home to the Father's house. I hope that you do, for in his eternal arms you will find the Father of your dreams.

In conclusion, I pray that "the God of our Lord Jesus Christ, the glorious Father, may give you the Spirit of wisdom and revelation, so that you may know him better" (Eph. 1:17 NIV). Amen.

Do you have a story about your personal journey to the Father's house that you'd like to share? I'd love to read it! E-mail it to me at: mary@marykassian.com, or send it to the following address:

Alabaster Flask Ministries
P.O. Box 57176
2020 Sherwood Drive
Sherwood Park, Alberta
Canada T8A 5L7

Conclusion

JUST ACROSS THE STREET from the house where I grew up in Canada is a ravine called Mill Creek, which flows toward the deep valley of Edmonton's North Saskatchewan River. In the winter, when it freezes to a depth of a couple of feet, the ravine is safe to walk and skate on. When I was young, my brothers and I spent many dusky winter afternoons skating, playing hockey, and pulling sleds across the surface of the ice. But in the spring we were forbidden to go to the creek because of the extreme hazard.

You see, the ice melts from the bottom up, so it's difficult to tell how much has melted underneath. Though the ice looks deceptively the same as it did in winter, under the surface, spring has begun its work. The ice can be thick in some areas but thin in others. If a child were to step on it, the thin portions might crack and give way, plunging the child into the frigid flowing waters. Every spring schools, parents, and media warn children of the danger, and signs are posted at the edges of creeks and lakes.

One spring, despite repeated warnings, an eleven-year-old boy, Jordan, his eleven-year-old friend, Mark, and Mark's six-year-old brother clambered down through the dense thickets and poplar trees to play in a culvert beneath a century-old wooden trestle in Mill Creek Ravine. The boys had taken only a few steps inside the culvert when the ice violently cracked and gave way, sending Jordan and the six-year-old tumbling into the chilly water. Mark pulled his young brother out and then looked for a branch to extend to his friend. Seconds later, when Mark turned back, Jordan was gone, swept under the ice by the swift-flowing current of the spring melt. Horror stricken and terrified, Mark and his brother ran home. They told no one. Jordan did not come home that night. It was not until police questioned his classmates at school the next day that Mark broke down and confessed.

Firemen and policemen used chainsaws, augers, and picks to break through the ice below the culvert. Commercial divers probed the murky spring melt-water. The task was extremely dangerous. The ice, which ranged in thickness from eight inches to five feet, was unstable. The water was frigid and could quickly cause hypothermia. Furthermore, the task was extremely tedious. Jordan's body might have been trapped anywhere between the culvert and the place where the ravine spilled into the river two miles downstream. Late that afternoon the search was officially postponed until the ice thawed. But that wasn't good enough for Jordan's father.

The following morning his father returned with rented chainsaws and augers and broke through the ice in various spots, slowly working his way down the winding creek. With mirrors and flashlights he peered into air pockets between the ice and flowing water, hoping to catch a glimpse of his son. Wearing hip waders, he chipped away at the ice day after day, often with numb and bloodied hands. News of his dogged persistence aroused the compassion of the city, and dozens upon dozens of complete strangers came out to help. Day after day, dawn till dusk, the search continued. A week after the drowning, it was starting to look hopeless. Most of the helpers had given up. But though he showed signs of exhaustion, the father refused to stop looking. In an interview he explained, "I can't rest until I find him."

On the eighth day a spectator spotted Jordan's body jammed beneath a thick shelf of ice. A hush fell as his father waded into the creek, pulled his son's cold, stiff body from the water, held him close to his heart, and wept.

Like Jordan's father, our heavenly Father looks for us when we run away. He does not rest. He does not give up when all others have lost hope. Day after day he persists until he holds his wayward child in his arms. But unlike Jordan's father, our heavenly Father can bend over and breathe life into our stiff, frozen souls. He breathes again and again until our cheeks turn from blue to white to pink. He holds us close to his heart until our heart pumps blood and our limbs begin to move again.

Consider your relationship to your heavenly Father. Are you neglectful of him, playing by the side of the creek, unaware of the danger of the ice? Have you fallen into the chilling water? Are you being swept away in the current? Do you feel cold and numb? Are you aware of your need for him to hold you and breathe life into your spirit? Do you know and love your Father? Do you know how much he loves you and how he longs to hold you close?

I hope this book has helped you understand more about the Father's great love and has motivated you to move closer to him. For some of you, this journey has been a delight. For others, it was undoubtedly difficult as you began to face and unpack the painful emotions surrounding your relationship with your earthly dad. Some of you experienced significant growth and healing, while others were unable to completely extend forgiveness and blessing. For some this was the culmination of a long journey toward embracing God as Father. For others it was just the beginning. Regardless of your personal situation, I pray that you will continue to press ever deeper into the Father-heart of God. I pray, in line with the J. I Packer quote at the beginning of this book, that the thought of being God's child and having God as your Father will be the thought that prompts and controls your worship and prayers and your whole outlook on life, that it may be the desire that ignites, stirs, and sustains you. Press ever deeper, my friend! For it is only in the Father's house that you will find your heart's true home.

NOTES

Introduction

1. David Blankenhorn, *Fatherless America: Confronting Our Most Urgent Social Problem* (New York: Harper Collins Books, 1995), 1.

2. Ibid., 3.

3. C. S Lewis, *Mere Christianity* (Glasgow: William Collins Sons & Co. Ltd., 1942), 65.

Chapter 8, The Father Crowns You with His Love

1. Luci Shaw, *Polishing the Petoskey Stone: Selected Poems* (Wheaton, Ill.: Harold Shaw Publishers, 1990).

Part 3, Getting to Know God as Father: Father God Looks after You

1. Peter Kreeft, *Making Sense Out of Suffering* (Ann Arbor, Mich.: Servant Books, 1986), 129, 136.

Chapter 13, Father God Is Protective

1. John Piper, "A Vision of Biblical Complementarity: Manhood and Womanhood Defined According to the Bible" in *Recovering Biblical Manhood and Womanhood*, eds. John Piper and Wayne Grudem (Wheaton, Ill.: Crossway Books, 1991), 42.

Chapter 16, Father God Is a Generous Provider

1. J. I. Packer, *Your Father Loves You: Daily Insights for Knowing God* (Wheaton, Ill.: Harold Shaw Publishers, 1986), reading for May 5.

2. Richard J. Foster, *Prayer: Finding the Heart's True Home* (New York: Harper Collins, 1992), 181.

, *Clearing the Barriers That Hinder Your Relationship with God the Father*

1. Thomas A. Smail, *The Forgotten Father: Rediscovering the Heart of the Christian Gospel* (London: Hodder and Stoughton, 1987 ed.), 61–62.

Chapter 24, *Choosing to Believe the Truth about God the Father*

1. H. Norman Wright, *Always Daddy's Girl: Understanding Your Father's Impact on Who You Are* (Ventura, Calif.: Regal Books, 1989), 195–97.

Part 6, *In My Father's House*

1. J. I. Packer, *Your Father Loves You: Daily Insights for Knowing God*, reading for September 22.

Chapter 28, *The Joy of His House*

1. C. S. Lewis, The Weight of Glory (New York: Collier Books, MacMillian Publishing Company, 1949), 3–4.

Chapter 29, *Making Your Home with the Father*

1. Max Lucado, *The Great House of God: A Home for Your Heart* (Dallas, Tex.: Word Publishing, 1997), 3–4.

2. John Piper, *Desiring God: Meditations of a Christian Hedonist* (Portland, Ore.: Multnomah Press, 1986), 75.

3. A. W. Tozer, *The Pursuit of God* (Camp Hill, Pa.: Christian Publications, 1982), 14.